CHRISTIAN EDUCATION:

Principles & Practice

Stan E. DeKoven, Ph.D.

CHRISTIAN EDUCATION:
Principles & Practice

Dr. Stan DeKoven

Revised Edition 2016

ISBN 978-1-61529-173-1

Copyright © 1996 by Dr. Stan DeKoven

Vision Publishing
1115 D Street
Ramona, CA 92065
(760) 789-4700
www.booksbyvision.edu

All rights reserved.

This publication cannot be reproduced or copied, whole or in part, without the written permission of the author, except in brief quotations embodied in critical articles of review.

Foreword

Christian Education, especially education within the local church setting is a primary vehicle for the transmission of the Christian faith from generation to generation. Throughout the history of God's dealings with His people, He has used both formal and informal methods of instruction within the family and society in general, as the way of transmitting the truth of His revelation to mankind.

Education is vitally important in our present day. It has been under significant attack due to the various methods of secularization being espoused within Western culture.

The reaction to that secularization amongst members of the Christian community has been the development of many private Christian educational programs, many of which are of outstanding quality. These programs are meeting an identified need, which is recognized by both academics and parents alike. That need is to provide the specialized education and training experiences for children that will integrate historic Christian faith with active academic pursuits.

All educators are keenly interested in their quest for truth. They are also interested in the attainment of excellence by their students and assisting those students in developing a worldview that will enhance their daily life and strengthen them for their future life endeavors.

As Christians it is an abiding hope to assist students in the development of a solid evangelical Christian worldview. This philosophy of life will provide the student with the ability to integrate truth wherever it is found, and make proper spiritual application of what is learned within one's own life cycle. It is the intention of this book to assist many students and teachers to accomplish this lofty goal.

In this volume, the reader will review various principles of teaching and the educational process in general, as well as the overriding philosophy of Christian education. Further, the student and/or teacher will be able to apply these methodologies and understandings to enhance the educational process of children, youth and adults that they have the privilege of working with.

There is an apparent and growing need to train and develop educators who carry a burden for students and a heart for the Lord. Men and women in the field of education must be more than good people who share good things with their students. They must have a radical commitment to the discipleship process. The goal of this process discipleship process is to assist students in becoming everything that God has created them to be. This can include warriors for Christ, witnesses to the cross, communicators of the resurrection, a window through which the rest of humanity can look and see the Christ found in the word of God.

Christian Education is desperately needed throughout the United States, the Western world as well as the developing two-thirds world nations. It is with this intention that this book has been written; to bring understanding, revelation and knowledge of the Lord Jesus Christ and the ability to apply that knowledge, which is equivalent to wisdom, within the classroom setting.

Acknowledgments

I would like to acknowledge those who have been of significant assistance to me in my educational career over the years. Dr. Joseph Bohac is my former high school English teacher, and my second but by far most influential pastor. To this day he wishes he had shared more about English and less about the importance of the Holy Spirit (that was the primary topic of discussion during my English class in high school days) for my life and ministry. He combined education, counseling, and pastoral leadership in one package, which became an example of the possibilities for my life. I will always be grateful to him for being a positive and thoroughly human role model.

I would also like to acknowledge the teacher of teachers, and my dear friend, who is the international founder and Australian Director of Vision Christian College and the Vision International University Network of Colleges worldwide, Dr. Ken Chant. In my very best writing days my remotest hope is to write with the magnificent skill of Dr. Ken. His writings, oracle gift and life are an inspiration to myself and so many others who desire to communicate with clarity the wondrous Gospel of Jesus Christ.

There are many instructors that have had a major impact upon me in the educational process throughout my Bachelors, Masters, and Doctoral degree programs. Each one had a special part in my overall development as an academician and as an instructor. It is my hope that this work will be a blessing to them and a clear acknowledgment of their assistance over the years in my educational development.

Finally, I would like to thank the faculty and staff of Vision International University, along with the College and Seminary Network, who have encouraged me to continue in my writing endeavors. It is my hope that this book will be a blessing to our Bible College Network and for students in other Bible Colleges and Adult Education programs both nationally and internationally. It is for you that this book has been written.

Table of Contents

Foreword 3
Introduction The Purpose of Teaching 7
Section I The Purpose of Teaching: Christian Education and the Teacher 13
   Chapter 1 The Word and Teaching 15
   Chapter 2 The Dynamics of Teaching 25
   Chapter 3 The Prime Objective 43
   Chapter 4 The Firm Foundation 51
   Chapter 5 Philosophy of Christian Education 57
   Chapter 6 The Teacher In The Teaching Process 63
Section II The Process Of Teaching 73
   Chapter 7 From The Heart and Head 75
   Chapter 8 The Curriculum 81
   Chapter 9 The Methodology 89
Section II The Programs 107
   Chapter 10 The Big Picture 109
   Chapter 11 Children 127
   Chapter 12 Youth 143
   Chapter 13 Adults and Discipleship 149
Bibliography 165
Appendices 167

Introduction

The Purpose of Teaching

I still remember the look on my old professor's face when he asked me, "So you want to teach, do you?"

Well, I couldn't honestly say that I did, at the time. Certainly, I knew I wanted to be involved in education. I viewed counseling as one particular vehicle of discipleship where I could be effective in helping people with their Christian walk. Ultimately there was a part of me that had a desperate need to communicate the truth of the Lord Jesus Christ and to present information about him, in a forthright and systematic fashion. I knew that through effective educational communication it was possible to assist people in their spiritual journey. I'm not sure that I knew what I was getting into when I launched in the direction of counselor training and educational development. I knew one thing for certain; because of the call of God upon my life, it was inherent of me to obtain the requisite knowledge and understanding of the Word of God to impart the revelation of Jesus to whoever I came in contact with. I recognized that I had to have a clear and dynamic purpose behind my teaching ministry.

The first question that educators must ask themselves is "What is the purpose of teaching?" Probably the best and simplest answer to that question is "Because it is necessary in order for us to do the stated will of God." In Matthew 28:18-20 it says that, we are to teach people to obey everything that Jesus commanded his disciples to do. The focus of Jesus' entire life was on training his disciples. His teaching prepared them for their on going work, an extension of Jesus' ministry here on earth.

That same tradition has been passed on from that first generation of believers through each subsequent generation. A Christian educators focus is to teach, not just for the purpose of transmitting facts and figures to a student, but so that there will be personal transformation of that student into the image of Christ. Thus, our teaching should be impartational (see Romans 1:11 where *metadidomi,* giving over; produces *sterizo,* to turn resolutely and set fast), which means to bring transformation to the heart, mind and spirit of each individual student.

When true impartation occurs, transformation will be exhibited in the ability to obey the teachings or the commands of Christ. Through this process people become the disciples of Christ—those who are willing to be taught and learn so that they might become like the Master.

Like the Master

It has been said that, "It **takes a master** to produce a **Master**. Even Jesus refused to begin his ministry before his preparation was complete (compare Luke 2:49 and John 2:4). Most Christian Educators long to be an accomplished, master teacher like the Christ. To become a master teacher takes preparation. This includes the preparation of personal character, teaching methodology, understanding of the curriculum and methods of evaluation. These topics and many others will be covered within this volume.

The length of preparation time required to become a master teacher is in the hands of Almighty God Himself. Some especially gifted students may attend a College program, or schools of education, and because of their gifting teach with great effectiveness. There are many teachers who have never darkened the door of a bible college and yet, by the grace of God, are able to teach effectively, imparting revelational knowledge to members of Christ's Church. For most it takes time and hard work to prepare for a career of teaching. Positive professional preparation is vital in light of the continuous challenge of molding young minds and hearts for Christian service.

With A Plan

All current and emerging teachers must consider the question; "What is my plan for teaching?" What audience will become the primary focus of instruction? What style will be used to impact them? How will the instruction be presented? Most new teachers will attempt to emulate the style of the many instructors they have encountered in their life. But truly, "one size does not fit all!"

If the teacher will submit themselves to the Lord and to his process of training and development, what will emerge is their own unique and effective style. At the same time, one must never forget that there are certain and specific characteristics to be found within each and every "master teacher." If a new teacher will apply solid principles of teaching, systematically, to their own walk with God and to their teaching methodology, they will become far more effective within the classroom setting.

In this book there are several significant subjects that will be covered in great detail. They are listed in the table of contents. They have been broken down into three primary sections. The first section discusses The Purpose of Teaching: Christian Education and the Teacher. If an educator does not know what their purpose is, as well as how to set proper aims and goals, they will be ineffective in their professional role.

The second section discusses The Process of Teaching. The basic characteristics of quality teaching methodology and of the teacher's heart are reviewed. Also, the organizational development of teaching curriculum, along with methodologies for teaching and specific techniques that have been proven to be most effective in various educational settings will be presented.

The third section presents The Programs often seen in Christian Education. Not only will the teaching of children be discussed, but also the education of youth and adults. The big picture of Christian Education from birth to grave is examined, plus the specialized needs of children, youth and adults in their educational environment. Finally, the reader will be provided appendices that provide additional information of benefit to the professional educator.

Christian Education is a wonderful endeavor. It is vitally needed. In fact, it is the second most desired service requested by missions around the world, after requesting a printed bible in their own language.

It is my hope that the readers of this book will be inspired to become both private and public school educators. God has called every believer to be salt and light in the world. Wherever God has placed a teacher, whether in Sunday School, as a bible college instructor, a high school, junior high or elementary school in public or private setting, all need to have a clear understanding of the principles of Christian Education. The art form of Christian education is to learn to apply the principles of effective teaching for the edification of the learner. May God bless each student/teacher as they read and study and use this book to inspire teachers to greater preparation for this most dynamic ministry.

"The ideal condition would be, I admit, that men should be right by instinct; but since we are all likely to go astray, the reasonable thing is to learn from those who can teach."
Sophocles, Antique 1720

Section I

The Purpose of Teaching: Christian Education and the Teacher

"How can a young man keep his way pure? By keeping it according to Thy word. With all my heart I have sought Thee; Do not let me wander from Thy commandments. Thy word I have treasured in my heart, that I may not sin against Thee. Blessed art Thou, O Lord; Teach me Thy statutes. With my lips I have told of All the ordinances of Thy mouth. I have rejoiced in the way of Thy testimonies, As much as in all riches. I will mediate on Thy precepts. And regard Thy ways. I shall delight in Thy statutes; I shall not forget Thy word." Psalm 119:9-16

Chapter 1

The Word and Teaching

Teaching is the primary vehicle for the transmitting of cultural truth and biblical revelation from generation to generation. Throughout God's dealings with His people, He has commanded them to know the commandments and to teach them, so that all might live the commandments in daily experience. This process is to continue from generation to generation. This section briefly reviews some of the scriptural passages that provide an understanding of the need to teach. The special importance that God's Word places on the teaching ministry is elucidated.

In Psalm 143:10 the Word of God says, *"Teach me to do thy will."* One of the primary purposes of teaching ministry is to assist people to know what the will of God is and then to do it. This teaching, as stated in Deuteronomy 4:9 begins from the earliest age. It says, *"We are to teach them to our children."* Teaching and training is a process that begins in the family long before a child comes into either a Sunday school, children's church or a private Christian school setting. It is the responsibility of the parents to teach their children and to teach them well.

To Win the Hearts

Evangelism is one of the focuses of teaching. Psalm 51:13 states, *"I will teach transgressors your ways."* That was part of the heart of David, especially after he had experienced God's great mercy and forgiveness following his sin with Bathsheba. In I Timothy 3:2 it says, *"Now the overseer must be able to teach."* Everyone that is involved in leadership in any way within a local church setting should have the ability and the desire to teach. That does not mean that one is a gifted teacher, but is able to teach effectively so that others can learn the Word of God from them. In Titus 2:1 it states, *"you must teach what is in accord with sound doctrine* (or sound teaching)." It is not enough to just teach. It is essential to teach properly and systematically so that clear understanding of God's purposes for His people is gained. The teaching process is not to be mere rattling on about anything one feels. It is a process of imparting divine truth found within the Word of God, thus bringing change in the life of students.

To Equip the Saints

One of the primary scriptures that emphasizes the importance of teaching in the Christian church is Ephesians 4:11. In this verse Paul the Apostle teaches that the five-fold ministry, Apostles, Prophets, Evangelists, Pastors and Teachers are all necessary components in the ministry of perfecting the saints or bringing them to Christian maturity. Included in the list are pastors and teachers, who both have a primary focus of teaching. However, the entire five-fold ministry, as elders, must be able to teach, imparting relevant truth from God's precious word.

Paul continued his teaching to his son in the Lord, Timothy, that a primary duty of a pastor was to give himself to the reading of the scripture, as well as to preaching and to teaching (I Timothy 4:13). These were no doubt Timothy's primary gifts, provided to him by God through the prophetic word before being commissioned into full-time ministry.

Finally, in I Corinthians 12:28 teaching is presented as one of the ministry gifts to the church. Thus, within the New Testament church, teaching was and continues to be a vital function to be expressed within the local church.

That They Might Learn

The purpose of teaching should be to ensure that learning actually takes place. Just because someone is talking in front of a classroom does not mean that learning is actually occurring. Probably the greatest thrill that a teacher can have is to see the light go on in a learner's mind. To see someone experience what is commonly called an, "Ah-Ha!" in his or her life is a marvelous joy. The "Ah-Ha" occurs when the student finally understands something that they had not previously understood. No real teaching has taken place unless truth has become relevant to the student, which becomes applicable to their life. That is why learning is incomplete until it has become a part of the students' repertoire of knowledge and experience.

II Timothy 3:7 says, *"Always learning but never able to come to the knowledge of the truth."* That is a tragedy that many people experience. They spend much time in reading, studying and learning (not experiential) but never applying it to a life of effective service.

Christian Educators are to be involved in sufficient personal and professional preparation so as to become effective transmitters of God's truth, to be applied by the student for life. In this regard, the word of God speaks clearly and profoundly. A teacher is to:

> *"Study to show ourselves approved unto God, a workman that does not need to be ashamed and who will rightly or correctly divide the word of truth."* (II Timothy 2:15)
>
> *"I know that we who teach will be judged,"* (James 3:1)
>
> *"They want to be teachers of the law but they do not know what they are talking about or what they so confidently confirm."* (I Timothy 1:7)

It is a very powerful responsibility for teachers to be effective in their calling.

For His Reward

It would be a great tragedy if after a life of teaching that we stood before the Lord to hear Him state that what we had taught was only wood, hay and stubble rather than gold, silver and precious stones.

> Hebrews 5:12 says, *"Though by this time you ought to be a teacher, you need someone to teach you the elementary truths of God's Word all over again."*

There are many ways to view this bible passage. Many have said that the "student" spoken of must have been dull or ignorant. Perhaps the teaching methodology was ineffectively presented, making the learning process for the student nearly impossible. If it was the Apostle Paul who was doing the teaching, the assumption of dull and ignorant could possibly[1] be assumed. However, not all teachers conduct their lessons with clarity and under the unction or the Holy Spirit. The conscientious teacher will seek to effectively and convincingly teach their charge with the goal of pleasing the Master.

Student Centered

When teaching, if the student is not learning, we dare not solely blame the student. It must be determined what possible weakness within the teacher may limit the effective communication of the truth so a student might clearly understand it. The teacher is responsible for the communication, which should flow from the integrity of the character of an instructor who is fully prepared.

Consistent Lifestyle

Teachers should be able to walk what they talk. If one is to be a teacher, he or she should first have mastered, or at least be in the process of mastering, the lessons that are to be taught. There is nothing more hypocritical than to teach principles that are not lived out in personal life. All leaders, and especially teachers, will be judged for their teaching, and should be an example to others of the lessons being taught. Every student is the teachers' customer. The

---

[1] It is true that on one occasion Paul, preaching what some have termed an "everlasting Gospel" put a young man to sleep, causing him to fall out a window to his death. (Acts 20: 7-10) However, in spite of this, it is apparent that Paul, being raised in the Pharisaical tradition and under the anointing of the Holy Spirit, must have been a most effective teacher of the Word of God.

teacher is to be a servant to the student, not a master of them. A master teacher is one who is like Christ. Jesus was willing to wash the disciples' feet. He gave His life for them. The servant focus of life wills to impart revelational truth of Christ so that ones' students can become better equipped than the teacher.

Always Learning

It is also important as a Christian Educator to always be a student. An educator must be fascinated with the learning process, for one never does obtain it all. The pursuit of knowledge should not be in vain, but focused to be constantly fresh and able to impart new truth and revelation to openhearted students. Therefore, when teaching, they teach out of a heart of love and compassion for the students. This is to be done with the recognition that every student will learn at a slightly different rate. Therefore, the teacher must be patient, fully aware of the needs of the individual and able to effectively teach in submission to the Holy Spirit and to the Word of God.

Teachers Empowered by God

Teaching God's word is a privilege of immense proportion. The joy of communicating eternal truths to God's people keeps many of us in the pulpit and classroom.

Teaching in a dynamic fashion to bring about life transformation and preparation for greater Kingdom service is our desire. As with any goal, it is helpful to remind us of our primary task and set our hearts again in the direction of God's greater purposes. With God's help we can fulfill our purpose through the wonderful and Spirit empowered process of the ministry of God's precious word.

Dynamics of Teaching

There are six (6) concepts that together provide key foundational principles of dynamic teaching. They include the call, commission, character, concern, craft and cry of the teacher.

The Call

The call to teaching the word of God is a high calling. God should initiate the call. The function of a called teacher can be seen in the role of the Prophet, Priest, Scribe and Parent in the Old Testament, demonstrated in the ministry of Moses and Ezra (Deuteronomy 6 and Ezra 7:10). To be effective in teaching ministry at any level of service we must have a sense of God's divine favor or call to the position. A lack of call can create great frustration in the difficult work of educating the unwilling.

The Commission

Jesus and Paul were both identified as teachers. God commissioned each for the task of discipleship ministry. There are other gifts to the Body, discussed in Ephesians 4: 11,12, I Corinthians 12/14 and Romans 12, the chief purpose of each being to edify the church and bring it to maturity. Whatever level of teaching role, the bringing of men and women to full maturity in Christ, conforming them to his image is the goal. This can only be done as people come face to face with the living Christ. This is to be consistently accomplished through our teaching ministry, which brings transformation of their heart and mind from glory to glory (2 Corinthians 3:18). The teaching ministry, accomplished primarily in the local assembly (Romans 12:3-8) is to be presented with grace and filled with divine life. Thus, the commissioned teacher must accept their high position, whether derived through local pastoral authority or directly from God, and walk in the authority and measure of faith God has provided. Our commission is a serious and sacred trust, not to be acted upon lightly.

The Character

Charisma (gift and influence) is a great blessing to those who have it. However, God is far more interested and concerned about the transference of character than charisma. Each man or woman standing before a gathering of people small or great cannot help but emit who they are to the students. Thus, the character of the teacher should be sterling solid and tested.

Paul the Apostle was most concerned about the character issue, reminding Timothy and Titus, his son's in the Lord, of the importance of a fully consecrated life (I Timothy 2:2-3, Titus 1:5-9, 11, 2: 1-10). His desire was to see those placed in leadership committed to a life of piety and purity so their teaching might not be tainted by an inconsistent life.

The Concern

Teachers must be concerned with the proper application of the word of God, above all else. It is tragic to hear how sloppy some Pentecostal and Charismatic leaders can be with the word of truth. There is no excuse for inadequate research or the borrowing of spiritual cliches from other preachers. The purpose of teaching is to learn. Learning does not occur until the student can apply the word of God to their life.

Further, the teachers concern is the change of a pupil, both in terms of maturity and a progression of growth as outlined in 2 Peter 1:1-11. Of course, the highest goal is Agape, God's love demonstrated in compassionate living.

The Craft

A craftsperson is an expert with the ability to do something at a level of other experts in a chosen field. It is not the customer that determines the expert, but other experts of peers in the same field. Though there will always be different levels of ability amongst teachers (craftspeople), all true craftspeople will have a similar foundation, and a desire to always demonstrate excellence in their craft.

To become an expert teacher, we must be people of scholarly study (2 Timothy 2:15), of God's word (2 Timothy 3:14-17), with a passionate vision (Habakkuk 2:1-3, 14) to see God's word communicated in a systematic fashion (Acts 11/19) under the anointing of the Spirit of God (Luke 4). Our ability to communicate the word effectively should grow year by year, as we study diligently and practice daily. Further, when we allow true master teachers to assist us and humbly receive their peer review, we will grow in grace and expertise.

The Cry

The cry of my heart is that of the Apostle Paul. It could well be the cry of us all. That cry is that Christ would be formed in every student. Much has been said of late regarding everyone having a spiritual father or being a spiritual son. There is a virtue in having a mentor orchestrated by the Holy Spirit, as with Moses and Joshua, Elijah and Elisha, Paul and Timothy. However, a danger in the spiritual adoption process includes the natural human element of control, domination and hierarchy. Rather than seeking disciples after ourselves (see 1 Corinthians 3:1-9) we are to seek disciples we can lead toward Christ. To see the life of Christ, beginning with evangelism and continuing until maturity, manifest in the lives of God's people should be our greatest thrill.

All of us who have been called, commissioned, etc., to the ministry of teaching are truly blessed. We love the Word, are given insights by the Holy Spirit and are given opportunity to communicate the word with fruitful results in the lives of our students. Be encouraged! Your role is vital, your responsibility awesome, and the divine ability (grace) of God is amply available to fulfill our purpose for his Kingdom sake.

"To teach is to learn twice."
Joseph Joubert (1754-1824)

"A teacher affects eternity; he can never tell where his influence stops"
Henry Brooks Adam, The Education of Henry Adams, 1907

Chapter 2

The Dynamics of Teaching

In the first chapter we began to look at some of the basic biblical principles and Scriptural references relating to teaching. Only a brief overview was presented; there are many other scriptures that could be applied to the teaching profession. This chapter will review six primary aspects of a biblically called teacher. Both Old and New Testament models will be presented with some scriptural dynamics of teaching for your consideration.

The Teacher Called

The Old Testament presents several models of men who were primarily teachers. The first and most important is the parent. Deuteronomy 6:4 and beyond speaks about the responsibility of the parent, especially the father, as a role model for the teacher within the Old Testament. In many families today the role of the teacher has been fully delegated to the mother. It is often true that the mother has significantly more time for the teaching and training of the child. But the father is still seen as responsible for the assurance that the teaching and training of children from a biblical perspective is maintained within the home.

As God's progressive revelation was unveiled in the Old Testament, specialized leaders where raised up who were able to effectively impart the truth of God's Word to his people. They included the scribe, the priest and the prophet.

The Scribe

Scribes were writers or secretaries, primarily men, who copied the sacred scriptures and other important documents. As will be discussed fully in reference to the life of Ezra, the scribe was given the task of copying parchment pages in perfect detail. No mistakes were allowed, or the scribe would have to destroy the copy and start again. Further, well trained scribes, since they were so intimately knowledgeable of the Holy Writ, would be called upon to expound its' truth to others. The scribe fulfilled a most important role in Old Testament history.

The Priest

The priest was the religious and ceremonial leader in the Old Testament era. They functioned in an intermediary role between the people of God, conducting sacrifices and bringing worship to the Lord. They also provided instruction, especially during the times of feasts, fastings and festivals, which were part of the life experience of the Jews. They were responsible for the application of scripture copied by the scribes, and the carrying forth of the "thus saith the Lord" of the prophet.

The Prophet

The prophet or seer were men and women called by God to hear and proclaim the will, purpose and intention of God. The prophets, often working or traveling in bands known as the school of the prophets, focused on proclaiming the Word of righteousness and the judgments of God for the nations of Israel and Judah. Their intensity was most problematic to a King living in sin, and their proclamations brought hope and assurance to the righteous servant.

Ezra

One of the best models of an Old Testament teacher who thoroughly prepared himself for the ministry of teaching is seen in the life of Ezra.[2] Ezra was a young man, raised in a time of captivity for the children of Israel. The great days of the kingdom of David and Solomon had long since passed and the children of Israel, due to their disobedience to the purpose of God were held in captivity in

---

[2] For more on the life of Ezra, see the book, "Keys to Successful Living", by Dr. DeKoven.

the nation of Babylon. In the seventh chapter of the Book of Ezra we find a fascinating picture of Ezra's preparation. Verse six states that *"Ezra was a scribe, skilled in the Law of Moses...and the hand of the Lord his God was upon him."* With God's favor (grace, good hand) upon his life, he set himself in a direction of great destiny.

Ezra, being a scribe, would have been required to pay very close attention to detail. Historically, a scribe had to transcribe the word in perfect order for it to be acceptable. Any mistake made would necessitate the destruction of the page he was working on. Ezra would have learned to become a skilled craftsman, paying close attention to small details to ensure that his labor was not in vain. This is a characteristic of most good educators. They do not allow distractions that could prevent them from fulfilling their mission to come between their educating of children, young people or adults.

Christian Educators must have a sense of mission and purpose about what they do. Whether an administrator or a teacher, there must be a sense of ones' own destiny, of a calling to this profession. Many classroom teachers, who because of the bureaucracy of the school, or simply because they have lost their sense of focus, are unfortunately miserable in their chosen field. One cannot help but translate that same sense of dissatisfaction to the students within a classroom.

Set One's Heart

Referring to verse 10, Ezra had purposed in his heart to prepare himself for effective service. *"Ezra had set his heart to study the law of the Lord and to practice it and to teach God's statues and ordinances in Israel."* There are three primary purposes that Ezra set his heart towards. First he set his heart to study the law of the Lord.

As a Christian Educator the first and foremost responsibility is to develop a relationship with the Lord based upon a clear and thorough understanding of God's Word. It is essential to fix or set one's heart on a thorough knowledge and understanding of the things of God so as to properly transmit God's principles within a classroom setting.

To Do

Secondly, Ezra was to practice what he was learning from the Word of God. This practice was actually two-fold. First, he was going to do or obey the things that he was learning as he studied the law of God. Secondly, and equally as important, he was going to practice his area of ministry until he perfected it. That's one of the reasons why educational programs require student teaching as well as continuing education; to ensure that an educator remains sharp in their educational pursuits and in their ability to transmit truth within a classroom, or as a leader over an educational institution. Thus the practice is something that continues for the entirety of life. We can and should always be striving for improvement in knowledge and ability to communicate it effectively.

Third, his focus was not merely to learn God's laws and his ministry for his own sake, but so that he could one day teach the truth to God's people when he returned to Israel. In like manner, teachers need an equal sense of purpose and plan, to impart knowledge received though years of preparation for the blessing of Gods' people and the honoring of God Himself.

The Overriding Plan

The overriding plan of God for teaching is presented in Deuteronomy 6 where a picture of God's intention for education is revealed.

> Deuteronomy 6:1-9 says, *"Now this is the commandment and the statues and the judgments which the Lord your God has commanded me to teach you. That you might do them in the land where you are going over to possess it. So that you and your son and your grandson might fear the Lord your God to keep all of His statues and His commandments which I command you all the days of your life. And that*

your days may be prolonged. Oh, Israel you should listen and be careful to do it that it may be well with you and that you may multiply greatly just as the Lord the God of your fathers has promised you in a land flowing with milk and honey. Hear O Israel, the Lord is our God, the Lord is One. Ye, shall love the Lord your God with all your heart, with all your soul and with all your might. These words which I am commanding you today, shall be on your heart and you shall teach them diligently to your sons and shall talk of them when you sit in your house, and when walk by the way and when you lie down and when you rise up. You shall bind them as a sign on your hand and they shall be as frontlets on your forehead. You shall write them on the door posts of your house and on your gates."

God commanded through Moses that the teaching ministry be a primary function within the family and all of society. To know who God is, to love the Lord God with all of one's ability and to know how to live life to its fullest, based upon God's precepts, is the highest good. That is still the goal for modern times as Christian educators. Part of the purpose for communicating God's truth is to create an understanding in the students as to what God's purpose is for them, a purpose divinely determined from the beginning of time.

Also In the New

In the New Testament, the most comprehensive picture of God's plan for education is modeled through the life of Christ. In John 3, Nicodemus made a very profound statement when he said,

"For we know that you are a teacher sent from God for no one could do the miracles that you do except God was with them."

God was with Christ, God was in Christ, and Christ is God. The primary focus of Christ's ministry was that of discipleship or the transference of God's plan and purpose from his life into his disciples. When they were finished with their educational program, the three and a half years they spent with Jesus here on earth, the vision was for them to pick up and carry on the mantle or tradition established by Christ. With this mantle they would be able to fully communicate everything that they had been taught and to do everything that Jesus had done in the same way and with the same measure that Jesus himself did.

That should be the philosophical focus of every educator. The education transmitted to a child or adult should produce life experience with practical application. When a child has completed a class or educational program, they should be able to take what they have learned and be able to apply it to their lives. Thus they will be able to effectively develop their own potential in the Lord.

Not only was teaching the focus of Jesus' ministry but it became that of the Apostle Paul as well. In the Book of Acts, Paul joins the Apostle Barnabas, sitting at Barnabas' feet as an assistant instructor. His tutelage continued for a full year, where they jointly taught the disciples in the principles of Christ. It was in Antioch that believers in Jesus Christ were first called Christians. They must have had a fairly effective teaching program for such a visible change of character to occur. A good assumption is that Paul and Barnabas taught everything that Barnabas had learned while he sat at the feet of the Apostles in Jerusalem, prior to his being sent to spy out Antioch (Acts 11). Later the Apostle Paul continued in the same tradition. In the city of Ephesus (Acts 19), he focused his ministry on the disciples who followed him, and for two years he taught them. They rented a facility called the School of Tyrannus and daily instructed the disciples. What did he teach? Everything Barnabas and he taught in Antioch, which was a continuation of everything that the Apostles taught in Jerusalem. This in turn was essentially everything that Jesus taught and modeled to them. This dynamic process, one generation teaching the next the plans and purposes of God, continues at some level in today's Christian community.

The New Covenant Goal

In I Timothy 1:5 we read,

"But the goal of our instruction is love from a pure heart and a good conscience and a sincere faith."

Paul's goal in teaching Timothy was to transform his life, to change his priorities. Timothy was one of the primary disciples of the Apostle Paul, nurtured through Paul's teaching ministry. In this verse, the goal of his instruction is presented. Paul's goal became the goal of Timothy's teaching ministry at Ephesus. The first and most important goal was love, which flowed from a pure heart. Secondly, a good conscience or developing the mind of Christ was an essential goal, and third, a sincere faith, or a faith which was to be openly proclaimed by committed saints.

Pure Heart

Paul's focus of teaching was not just to stimulate the intellect or to provide facts and figures, but to ensure that a process of the purification of one's heart would occur. The love of God was to be seen and expressed in the life of the disciple. True love is to flow from a purified heart or one that has been changed by an encounter with the Spirit of God through the Word of God.

Good Conscience

A good conscience would indicate that through the process of the teaching ministry and the study of God's Word, a change would begin to occur in the thought life of the believer. This change occurred as they looked into the mirror of truth found in God's Word. As they looked or gazed in the mirror of truth, comparing their life to the word of God, areas of deficiency in need of correction would be revealed. As confession of areas of sin or failure is accomplished and repentance of them is done, the process of change takes effect. Ultimately, this process creates a clean and clear conscience, free from guilt and anxiety because of past mistakes or sin.

Sincere Faith

Finally, a sincere faith needs to be developed. This literally means a faithfulness to the task that God has called us to. Whatever educational program that a student is involved in, the hope is that when they have completed it, they will be faithful to perform what they have been trained to do. It is not enough to learn something without application. Jesus taught with an eternal focus in mind. What the disciples saw Christ do, they did. Paul worked from the same central concept. It is vitally important for teachers as leaders to emphasize theory, theology and effective practices, faithful to the knowledge and skills learned over time.

Gifts Needed

In the dynamics of teaching, a teacher should be called and commissioned with a sense of purpose. Part of that commissioning can be seen in Ephesians 4:11-12 where it describes the five-fold ministry and the purpose of these gifts of Christ. All of the five listed, the apostles, prophets, pastors, evangelists and teachers are to be active teachers, ministering the revelation of Jesus Christ. These are gifts, given by Jesus to the church, and are for the perfection or the maturing of the saints of God until all come into the unity of faith, able to fulfill their destiny in the Lord.

Romans 12:6 states,

"in the church there are various gifts that differ according to the grace given to us. Let us therefore exercise them accordingly. If prophecy according to the portion of faith, if service, in his serving, or he who teaches, in his teaching, or he who exhorts, in his exhortation", etc. (NAS)

In other words, ones teaching ability is going to be determined by the measure of God's grace given. Not everyone is going to have the same level of authority of teaching in the Body of Christ. A Sunday School teacher functioning according to their God given authority need never be ashamed. The Lord only requires us to walk in the gifting and anointing that is provided by God. In fact, to try to teach at a level above or different from where God has called would remove us from the center of God's will. In all teaching, it must be accomplished with a godly goal in mind and within the confines of our gift and authority.

The Biblical Perspective

Again, as emphasized in earlier portions of this text, all instruction should be done either within the home or the auspices of the local church. This does not say that other institutions are not serving the Lord. The primary locus of control of the educational process should be found within the confines of either the family or the local church. The teacher must be able to teach to the best of their ability as commissioned by the Lord, according to the grace that God has given and according to the measure of faith that He has provided. Whether one is five-fold ministry or has the gift, ability and desire to teach, they need to do so to the best of their ability as commissioned by the Master Teacher Himself.

The Teachers Character

When considering the dynamics of teaching, the discussion revolves around the flow of knowledge, wisdom and understanding that comes from one person; the teacher. The teachers' role is to transmit as effectively as possible to the individual student within a private or a group setting the truths being espoused. As such, there is always going to be transference of the heart and mind, or the character of the individual teacher to the students.

In the Word of God, whether it be a prophet or an evangelist, an apostle or whoever was doing the teaching, there was always an assumption that they were a person of proven character. Those that were found to lack integrity in life practice, or lived an inconsistent lifestyle, were justifiably seen as hypocrites. Christians were warned not to listen to them. However, to properly evaluate a teachers' integrity, it is important to have a working understanding of what the character of a teacher should be.

The best picture of the qualifications for leadership in general, and teachers specifically, is found in I Timothy 3. It is here that the characteristics for a deacon and elder are prescribed. All instructors should be able to fulfill the requirements found within God's Word for a deacon or an elder. A parallel of this teaching is found in Titus 1:5-9.

Summarized here are the core characteristics of a teacher in terms of the level of their heart responsibility. Other scriptures written by the Apostle Paul for edification are also presented.

The Sum Total

This summarization does not cover every aspect of the qualities required for a Christian Educator, but provides a good launching point. In I Timothy 3, the characteristics include: one who is above reproach or dishonor in the world. Further, someone that is faithful in their relationships, especially their relationship with their spouse. A leader must be prudent and careful or wise in their dealings, temperate, respectable, hospitable. Obviously, they should have the ability to teach unhampered by personal habits such as being highly argumentative, contentious, addicted to substances or other compulsive behaviors. One characteristic of an excellent teacher is that they tend to be gentle and patient. They are able to manage their own household well and have their life well ordered (not perfect). Further, they have had their lives and abilities tested over time. Of course, the adage to not be a novice must be balanced with not being despised for being young. Age is not the issue, but maturity and ability for leadership is the key. A leader, and by definition a teacher must be a person of good reputation, have dignity with an ability to speak the truth while living according to the principles they teach.

Further, one of the primary characteristic of a disciple and leader, especially in teaching, is that of faithfulness (2 Timothy 2:2). Faithfulness is required, to the task of teaching and to the pupils being taught. It should go without saying that a teacher must be a hard worker, not self-willed or given to extreme mood swings. They should love what's good (especially good effort & scholarship). A good teacher must be sensible, just, devout, under self-control, and able to exhort or encourage as well as to correct. The fruit of the Holy Spirit should be evident in their lives in increasing measure.

Finally, the bible states that it is the older women that are to teach the younger women; the older men to teach the younger men (Titus 2). Through the generations there is a process of transference of knowledge and wisdom as the older teaches the younger the principles of life. Of course, as teachers we need only be a step or so ahead of our students to effectively impact their lives. The principles of God's word are to be applied generously from generation to generation, contextualized to the needs of the culture.

The character of a teacher should be proven. To prove someone's character, we must be able to spend time with him or her to see how he or she actually functions under stress. This is not to suggest that a teacher has to be perfect, no one would ever qualify if perfection was the rule and necessity. But, a teacher should be working toward living a life which is consistent, faithful, solid and stable. Unfortunately, character is not often rewarded, even in teachers. In fact, it is the more flamboyant and outrageous which seem to receive the highest level of commendation. Teachers are responsible to transmit, not just information, but wisdom, knowledge and understanding from the Word of God and be an example of what a Christian should be.

The Teachers Concern

The concern of a teacher should always be the student. But, not the student first, because the primary responsibility is first to the Lord and then to the student. 2 Peter 1 presents a picture of the responsibility or the concern of the teacher. In verses 1-11 Peter expresses his heart for teaching and for the transmission of life and character to those that were under his tutelage.

Beginning with the second verse it says,

> *"Grace and peace be multiplied to you, in the knowledge of God and of Jesus our Lord. Seeing that his divine power*

> *has granted to us everything pertaining to life and godliness through the true knowledge of Him who called us by His own glory and excellence. For by these He has granted to us His precious and magnificent promises in order that by them you might become partakers of the divine nature having escaped the corruption that is in the world by lust. Now for this very reason also supplying all diligence in your faith, supply moral excellence. In your moral excellence, knowledge; and in your knowledge self-control; and in your self-control, perseverance; and in your perseverance, godliness; and in your godliness, brotherly kindness; and in your brotherly kindness, love. For if these qualities are yours and are increasing they render you neither useless or unfruitful in the true knowledge of our Lord Jesus Christ. For he who lacks these qualities, is blind or short sighted having forgotten his justification from his former sins. Therefore, brethren be all the more diligent to make certain about his calling and choosing you, for as long as you practice these things you will never stumble."*

This is a very powerful passage of scripture. It could easily be applied to ones' growth and character as a leader in general. This passage presents a progression of process, taking students step by step towards ever more pleasing behavior to the Lord. The progression will ensure that they become conformed to the image of Christ, becoming what God intends, which is ultimately expressed as *agape'* love. The process includes diligent application of principles of faith that will lead to moral excellence, which will lead to knowledge and self-control, perseverance, godliness, brotherly love and true love. These are qualities that a teacher should be looking for and attempting to either impart to or bring out of their students, regardless of whether they are children, youth or adults. Some would look at these as simply lofty goals. However, they should be the primary concern of every Bible teacher, or any teacher in any Christian oriented class setting. The educator is tasked to create a Christian worldview, which includes the manifestation of these principles in their life.

To Grow Up

Referring back to Ephesians 4:11-12, the concern or goal of instruction is to bring students to maturity. The focus of the teaching ministry of the Apostle Paul was precisely that. It was certainly the focus of Christ. If the focus was perfection, then both Jesus and Paul failed miserably. None of their students were paragons of perfection. Their goal and ours is not perfection but maturity. Maturity can be seen in the ability to rightly divide or understand God's truth and transmit it in spite of human frailties. Having the same concerns that God has for the students will assist us to remain on track. The goals of instruction go far beyond teaching the brightest to shine (which they no doubt will do with us or without us) or have the highest grade point average, but to ensure that the character of God is being formed in the hearts of his people. The educators concern will be the focus of the educational ministry.

The Teachers Craft

When speaking about the teachers' craft, we are referring to the tools of the trade. The tools available to us as instructors include time spent in the preparation of the subject matter being communicated within the classroom setting.

2 Timothy 2:15 speaks of a prime purpose of the teaching of the Word of God.

> *"Study to show thyself approved unto God, a workman that needs not to be ashamed, rightly dividing the word of truth."*

An instructors study must be with a focus. The focus is to understand the Word and communicate it with clarity and conviction. This brings the reader to the next point, which is the Word itself.

2 Timothy 3:14-17 says, *"You however, continue in the things which you have learned and become convinced of knowing from whom you have learned them and that from childhood you have known the sacred writings which are able to give you the wisdom that leads to salvation through faith which is in Christ Jesus. All scripture is inspired by God and profitable for teaching, for reproof, for correction, for training in righteousness that the man of God might be adequate, equipped for every good work."*

The word adequate referred to here simply means to be equipped or fully trained, able to apply the craft of education within an organized structure. The Word of God is able to change the hearts and minds of men and women. That is why we teach God's Word. Our focus is to first learn and then transmit what is learned with accuracy so others may comprehend the fullness of meaning.

Habakkuk 2:1-3 states, *"I will stand on my guard post and station myself on the rampart; and I will keep watch to see what He will speak to me, and how I may reply when I am reproved. Then the Lord answered me and said, 'Record the vision and inscribe it on tablets, that the one who reads it may run. For the vision is yet for the appointed time; It hastens toward the goal, and it will not fail. Though it tarries, wait for it; for it will certainly come, it will not delay.'"*

Professional educators must have vision. The vision includes the ability to see students differently than when they first began their academic sojourning. Many students, whether they be in a kindergarten class, a pre-school program, Head-start, a Bible college or even a liberal arts University, look like David's rag tag band when they first come to the classroom.

Teachers must have a vision for their students that will take the pupil far beyond their present level of knowledge to the place where God wants them to be. In order to do so, educators must clearly receive a vision from the Lord for the students' transformation through the revelation of the truth of the Word by the inspired instruction presented. Much prayer should be a part of the process. It helps to set aside quality time with the Lord, being willing to accept correction if the vision for the students is less than God's perspective. God can and will provide clear vision of the potential for each student being instructed.

Further, the Word says to *"write the vision, make it plain,"* or make it clear, *"so that those who read it will run with it,"* or proclaim it. The instructors' goal is to communicate their subject matter with sufficient clarity and inspiration for the student to proclaim the instruction to others. The hope is to take the most problematic students, those who present the greatest challenge, and impart to them a sense of hope and belief in themselves and their God. With this confidence the student will do more than ever thought. Part of our craft is to encourage the learner to learn, to show the individual student what they can and can not do, taking them beyond the level of present functioning. Thus, motivating the student to study and learn is a key to the teaching process. Motivation requires several components. These include the attitude of the learner toward him or her self (self-concept), the attitude of the learner toward the group (self-other concept), the attitude of the learner toward the teacher (the self-teacher concept) and the attitude of the learner toward the learning situation (the self-situation concept) Edge, pg. 55-57.

It is most helpful as an educational craftsman to write down the vision God will give for each student being taught. This personal touch takes time to do, but it is well worth the effort, as through the eyes of faith students outstretch the expected, of the student and the teacher. The vision must be positive, looking for the good and extracting from the students their honest best through the educational process. With positive effort, and by the grace of God, the student will grow in knowledge, understanding and wisdom. If we are professional in our approach, diligent in our application of proven teaching methodology, if our character and heart is right before the Lord with a focus to assist the student, positive results will be evident.

Systematic Instruction

In Acts 11 and later in Acts 19, Paul and Barnabas taught the disciples in a systematic and organized fashion. Their program of instruction was not haphazard or slipshod. Some might view the teaching ministry of Jesus as Laissez-faire, teach as we go type of instructional format. Nothing that Jesus did was by accident. The Father orchestrated his ministry. Jesus, in perfect obedience to the voice of His Father, taught His disciples in such a way that they internalized the Teacher as a model. This internalized model prepared them to effectively train others for full-time ministry. They were organized and systematic, beginning with foundational teachings and principles, building on these principles, line upon line, precept upon precept. Since all students begin at a slightly different baseline, understanding the relative strengths and weaknesses of the student becomes most evident. Some students will be very high in achievement and advanced in learned knowledge, some will be quite low and unprepared for the class being taught. It is the teachers' responsibility to organize the instruction and teach the material in a systematic fashion. The hope is to provide for each student the opportunity to learn at his or her highest possible level of achievement, moving forward from one foundation to another.

Pauline Model

The Apostle Paul was a most disciplined instructor. In his writings, Paul painstakingly transitions from one principle to another. Building slowly, precept upon precept, the reader is generally able to follow the progression of his thoughts (though even the Apostle Peter had difficulty with some of his letters). Teachers need to instruct with purpose and fluidity. To be fluid one must be organized and prepared. A part of the teacher's craft is to see the anointing of God and the authority that God gives, inherent in the role as teacher, be released on behalf of the student.

Matthew 28 speaks about the authority that was given to Jesus in heaven and earth, and was subsequently given to his disciples. Their commission was to go forth and make disciples of the nations. The process to follow included preaching the word of God, baptizing in the name of the Father, Son and Holy Spirit, then teaching the converted to do all that Jesus commanded, by the grace of God. God is with the teacher in the classroom as they submit themselves to the Lordship of Christ. If we are in a place of authority to teach students, then we do not have to gain the authority, but must act based upon God given authority. The teacher must assume their classroom authority. Thus, the professional educator begins a new class, not as the students' best friend, but as a mentor/teacher in control of the class. If the teacher is strong and structured in the beginning, it is always possible to lighten up later. The reverse is not always true. Along with the authority that God gives, the Lord will also provide unction or an anointing from the Holy Spirit. God's Word will never return void; it will never return empty. Thus, when teaching the Word of God, know that there is an anointing; an unction that is already on God's Word that is able to penetrate the hearts and minds of the most difficult student. The teacher should not let anyone, especially their students, minimize the instructional role within a classroom. God has given great authority to those called to teach His word, and gives an equal anointing to teach or to communicate truth so that it will effectively change the hearts and minds. Trust the process. If instruction is well prepared with God's help, if the teacher is commissioned with proven character and a concern for the student, what will ensue is an application of the craft of teaching, which will bring about positive results, pleasing to God and a blessing to the students.

"Education has for its object the formation of character."
Herbert Spencer (1820-1903),
Social Statics, Ch. 17, 4

Chapter 3

The Prime Objective

In teaching religious subjects, there are several principles and methods that must be learned. It is important to keep in mind what the prime objective of Christian education is. Listed here are eight primary objectives that will keep the teacher on track and ensure the establishment of a firm foundation for the children and/or adults that are being taught.

Number one, teachers are **interpreters of truth**. God has given a tremendous responsibility to educators, to know the Word of God, and to understand it sufficiently so as to interpret it's meaning properly from God's perspective to the students. This is no small assignment. We must be very, very cautious to ensure the correct communication of the word of God, and insure accuracy of the Biblical record, which would be pleasing to God. Thus, the study of hermeneutics and exegesis within the discipline of hermeneutics is essential for every educator. This is especially true for a teacher of the Word of God. In the modern era we live in, there are many helpful tools that have been developed to assist in the accurate understanding of scripture. From software programs for computers to various commentaries, concordances and lexicons, if one is willing to put in the time and energy to study properly, they will be able to "rightly divide" God's Word with clarity.

An interpreter of truth must know the truth. That is, a teacher must have an intimate relationship with the Lord Jesus Christ who is the truth and must be willing to take a fiduciary responsibility in communicating the truth accurately.

A second focus or prime objective is to **build Christian personality or character**. Theologically, the character of man or the likeness of God within man as God's creation was distorted or twisted (iniquity) through the fall of man. Because of this fact, every individual, from childhood on, needs to experience a saving knowledge of the Lord Jesus Christ.

When one is born again, the image of God is reestablished within the spirit, but the character or personality, which is developed and shaped primarily within the early formative years of childhood, still needs to be transformed. The process of change occurs by the renewing of the mind, which is to a large extent what the educational process is to accomplish. The teacher must be able to interpret scripture and impart truth, and in doing so bypass the understanding level of the intellect, allowing the truth to sink into the depths of the personality or character, so that the mind might be transformed into the image of Christ.

The transformation of character is not solely the responsibility of a teacher. Obviously that process should begin with parents. Further, there are many other people who impact the character of an individual students' life. However, the teacher is in a unique position to effect the students' character as the word of God is taught systematically. The goal being to make the student more Christ-like, manifesting the fruit of the Holy Spirit in daily conduct.

Thirdly, children become the **bearers of spiritual culture**. That is, they are the future demonstrators of Christlikeness. Developing a classroom environment with a positive spiritual climate and transmitting relevant truth to students is highly important. As children are taught they should bear the marks of the teacher in their hearts and behavior. Not that perfection is expected, but an ability to understand what a Christian culture is and communicate it to the world is the goal.

Christian culture is defined differently by different segments of society. Some qualities that are expected in children and young adults may not be realistic, or necessarily biblical. Therefore, one should be careful of what type of culture is being created in a classroom. Not all of what the church values as Christian can be justified biblically. The goal should be to develop in pupils a

Christian worldview that is in agreement with the full counsel of God's Word.

Fourth, recognize that a leader in education is to develop **disciples for kingdom living**. In reality, very few students are going to remain full-time within a Christian educational environment. In fact, all believers are to be salt and light in the world, able to live out the kingdom principles of righteousness, peace and joy in the Holy Spirit (Romans 14:17), in whatever environment they are placed in. This requires understanding and knowledge of what kingdom living is all about, the process of learning how to live by kingdom principles. It takes the experience of being in a non-Christian culture for one to demonstrate the difference in a Christians' lifestyle, different than the world because of what has been learned of Christ and His Word. Part of the prime objective of a Christian educational ministry is to ensure that believers are able to function well within a Christian culture, and equally able to live as Christians in a non-Christian or even hostile environment. Thus, every student becomes a transforming agent in society, while not becoming transformed by the world system.

The fifth prime objective for Christian education is to remember that the **subject matter that is taught is to be subordinate to the life that is being transmitted** to the student. Regardless the subject being taught, nor how fascinating or vital one thinks the subject matter to be, the objective is to prepare a student to fulfill their life goal and dream according to God's plan and purpose for their lives. Jesus said, *"wisdom is justified by all of her children,"* (Luke 7:35). The intent of Jesus' statement was that regardless of what others thought of him as a teacher, when the results of the teaching of his disciples were seen, his methods and relevance would be justified. The illumination of truth will not be perceived through the preponderance of pontification or because students have become parrots like the Pharisees. The proof of quality instruction will be seen in a marked difference in the students' character. When a student is able to demonstrate a Christian life that has become a testimony to the world of God's grace and goodness and the teaching program that they have been subjected to, teacher satisfaction can be enjoyed.

Sixth, the teachers' focus is to create in children or adults a fully rounded and **well-developed Christian worldview**. The Christian worldview that students develop, should not be that of a Greek oriented philosophical system. Simply, the Greeks (mind) focused on a dualistic viewpoint of the world. That is, that man was body and soul only. Thus, the world could be divided into secular and sacred. The belief is that the two should not mix. To a great extent this philosophical worldview has infiltrated educational systems and has even filtered down to the local church. There are many people who have had a born again experience and yet in their business world or personal relationships they live like the world. In the local church they appear to be wonderful, loving people. However, in the "real world" their Christian life seems null and void. In reality a Christian worldview should reflect the philosophy of the Hebrew children. Christians are grafted into Abraham's covenant. From a Hebrew worldview, which is more eastern than western in orientation, all things are spiritual. Every aspect of life and behavior should be effected by ones' belief system. Thus, all of life should be effected by Christian principles. For instance, our work should be governed by principles of proper business ethics according to the Word of God. In the educational system, the same would be true. Our relationships should be governed by the relationship with the Lord and by His Word. Thus, a persons' worldview effects or should effect every aspect of life. That is part of what an educator attempts to do through various educational programs. Whatever subject is being taught, or administered within a local church, the focus should be to assist the student at whatever level to obtain a crystallized Christian worldview.

Number seven is to **show God revealed**. That is, through the teachers' lifestyle as well as through their teaching, the goal is to make disciples, not specifically of the teacher, but ultimately of Christ. Students are to become quality men and women who have a revelation of who God is as revealed through Jesus Christ. For the teacher to show God revealed means to become a mirror image of Christ for the student. This will occur as God's Word is being taught, and as the life of the teacher is consistent with the teaching.

Further, the teacher is to assist the student to develop a similar understanding. The hope is that the student will internalize a natural process of asking themselves the question, what would Jesus do in a given situation? What would my instructor do, if they were faced with a similar situation that I am faced with? Hopefully, they will respond according to the worldview that has been imparted to them, a view filled with the principles of kingdom living found in God's Word.

The final prime objective for Christian education is to **impart knowledge and wisdom** into the student so that they will **develop the fear of the Lord**. In western society there has been an extreme breakdown in respect for authority. Many educators advocate an open classroom setting, where students have equal authority to say whatever they feel and do whatever they want. This frequently causes a defying of the basic rules of propriety, resulting in a decrease in the student's ability to gain knowledge and understanding which will lead to wisdom, which is the fear of the Lord.

One of the prime objectives for Christian education is to teach discipline, self-control, and a respect for legitimate authority. All authorities that have been given by God through government and educational systems, should be shown double honor and respect, especially teachers. As a teacher, we must reinforce this reality to the students. Any teacher that would allow themselves to be subjected to an onslaught of disrespect from a student is simply asking for trouble. Ultimately teachers must be willing to bring correction and discipline to a student, even if it means having them removed from the class. For the sake of the whole, sometimes it is necessary to eliminate the one. Knowledge and understanding leads to wisdom or the ability to apply God's Word and the principles that are being taught within the life of the student. The basis or the ultimate prime objective and the foundation for the learning process is awe or respect for God, His Word and His servants.

Lessons From Early Jewish Education[3]

"It is not an overstatement to say that the Jewish people have had a reverence for education unequaled by any people in the history of the world." So begins the assertions of Dr. Paul A. Kienel the founder and President Emeritus of the Association of Christian Schools International. Dr. Kienel describes some of the most cogent aspects of the Jewish tradition of education, which are applicable to our times. In the article he quotes the famous Jewish historian Flavius Josephus, who lived at the time of Christ, who said, "our ground is good, and we work it to the utmost, but our chief ambition is for the education of our children."

The commitment of the Jewish religions to their children is historic. The commitment to children can be seen in their esteem given to their teachers. The following are popular sayings at the time of Christ:

"Respect your teachers as you would God."[4]

"The teacher precedes the father; the wise man, the king."[5]

"If one's teacher and one's father is in captivity, one must ransom his teacher first."[6]

"What does God do during the fourth quarter of the Day? He sits and instructs the school children."[7]

Prior to the time of Christ, the teacher was esteemed with a high social standing, second only to the rabbinical scholar. By the time

---

[3] Lessons From Early Jewish Education, Paul Kienel, Association of Christian Schools International "Christian Schools", Vol. 8, 28

[4] Frederick Eby and Charles Flinn Arrowood, The History and Philosophy of Education Ancient and Medieval, New York, Prentice Hall, 1940, P. 156

[5] Ibid.

[6] Baba Mezia II, 11. Quoted in Lewis Joseph Sherrill, The rise of Christian Education, New York, The Macmillan Company, 1944, P. 69

[7] Ibid., p. 50, Sherrill quotes Abhoda Zara 3 b.

of Christ, there was already over 480 synagogue schools in Jerusalem, the first being established by law 75 years before Christ. These schools were tax supported, had the primary text of the Old Testament scriptures and adhered to a very rigid schedule of year round instruction, with daily instruction from dawn until dusk.

"A study of Jewish education adds clarity to…Luke 6:40. Jesus said, "A disciple (student) is not above his teacher, but everyone who is perfectly trained will be like his teacher." It was the objective of every student in a Jewish school to become exactly like their teacher. A Jewish student not only acquired knowledge from his teacher but every characteristic of his teacher including hand gestures and voice inflection. Christian schoolteachers today might like the Jewish ruling that read: 'All manner of service that a slave must render to his master, a student must render to his teacher, except that of loosening his shoe.' The idea being that a student revered a teacher so much that he felt unworthy to loosen his shoe. Perhaps that is why John the Baptist said of Jesus, "There comes One after me who is mightier than I, whose sandal strap I am not worthy to stoop down and loose." (Mark 1:7)

In Israel, the focus of education was on preparing children for the next generation, the task being a central activity of society. In present times, we should have no less commitment.

*"Learning is not attained by chance,
it must be sought for with ardor
and attended to with diligence"*
*Abigail Adams,
letter to John Q. Adams,
May 8, 1780*

Chapter 4

The Firm Foundation

Christian education must begin from some specific foundational principles. Many additional and equally important principles will be discussed in the next chapter. The foundational principles that must be considered when developing educational ministry are extensions of the Word of God and personal character qualifications of the individual instructor. This chapter will discuss four primary foundational principles necessary to build a solid Christian educational ministry.

First, to have a firm foundation, teachers must have a clear aim for their educational ministry. That is, the teacher must have goals in mind that will have specific outcomes, which ultimately will include the establishment of the kingdom of God within the life of the individual student. According to Romans 14:17, the goal of all instruction is to produce righteousness, peace and joy in the life of every student that the teacher influences. Simply, students must learn to think right and live right, to know, understand and follow the basic precepts of God.

A specific goal or aim for an educator is to build a godly self-image in students. A godly self-image provides healthy self-confidence for the student to emerge, necessary for maximal learning. The hope is that the student will experience peace that comes from a right relationship with God and with their fellow man. Also, a teachers' hope is for them to experience joy. Joy comes when our students accomplish something thought to be above their capability to accomplish. So often, students will enter the classroom, (this is especially true in adult education) with fears about their ability to matriculate. However, with a positive and well-trained educator and the grace of God they can learn and grow. This creates a tremendous sense of exhilaration or joy within the student. Thus, teachers work towards desired outcomes that will include a positive attitude toward life, positive conduct in terms of understanding the way to live a godly life, how to treat their fellow man and new skills to be applied to their life consistently over time. Students properly trained will develop fruitful knowledge, right attitudes and skillful living, fully able to apply the principles they have learned within the classroom setting for the rest of their life.

Secondly, the student must learn a specific subject matter. That subject matter, regardless of what it is, should be suited to the aims of the class. Teachers must ensure that academic goals are realistic for the student and see to it that the curriculum will actually teach the student what they are supposed to learn. Having a specific goal or outcome in mind for a class, whether a seminar, a long-term class or a very short-term continuing education program is key. In light of that, the educational program and the subject matter should be adapted to the audience being taught. In some ways, a teacher must be able to teach to three audiences simultaneously, especially if they are teaching to a mixed group like a Sunday morning congregation. That is, they must be able to reach the child, the young man or woman as well as the adult inside every individual. They must be flexible in approach, able to instruct to cause growth towards maturity, regardless of the spiritual maturity of the students instructed. As educators, we must become adaptable to various audiences, able to present subject matter with the goal of accomplishing the aim for that student or for the classroom milieu.

Third, educators must organize themselves or develop a plan to accomplish the aims or goals that are set before them. Professional teaching will present material in a psychologically astute fashion. The material will be organized according to well-founded learning principles as discovered by such men and women as Piaget, Erikson, Montessori and others. Further, it is necessary to ensure that the subject matter taught is age appropriate presented to reinforce and enhance the normal learning processes for children, young people or adults. Children need rewards as a part of the teaching process. Since young children want to please adults, especially authority figures, educators can cooperate with that reality and use positive reinforcement or the lack of positive reinforcement (negative reinforcement) as one of the primary learning principles in classroom management.

Further, to utilize the ability of children to play and use creative energy and fantasy in the learning process is essential for success. Fantasy is not a negative. Being able to imagine is one of the gifts of childhood. Also, educators recognize the way children actually absorb information and the fact that they require repetition of material taught for full understanding to be gained. A skilled and creative teacher will take these learning principles and others and apply them with diligence in the classroom. These learning principles, which are beyond the focus of this book, must be followed in a judicious manner in order to ensure that adequate educational processes are actually occurring.

Relevancy

One of the major concerns Christian educators express in their dealings with young people and adults is how to make the educational process relevant. Relevance is accomplished through providing immediate interest in the topic and application of what is being learned. When young people, especially ages 14 to adulthood, are taking a course, they will ask themselves the simple question, "What can I use this information for?" In some ways this is one of the reasons that algebra is such a difficult topic for many. The primary problem with the subject is that there is little apparent relevancy or practical application of the course content. "How am I going to use this material to help me in regards to my future career, my high school graduation, or my college entrance?" The only reason that we usually hear for the importance of Algebra is that it helps the student to think more logically. Further, Algebra is a required course in order to graduate from high school and enter college.

Immediate application of learning is an important aspect of the educational process. Immediate meaning where the student can see light at the end of the tunnel in terms of the usage of the material being learned. In other words, the immediate reinforcement of studying drivers education is the soon ability to obtain a drivers license and hopefully drive. The immediate application of a course on ministry gifts or on marriage and family life is the ability to apply what is learned to life experience. So it is very important to find ways to make the curriculum relevant to the individual student for now and for their future.

Finally, a firm foundation is laid in education through the actual presentation of the material within the classroom setting. Every educator attempts to present information in an inspirational style. Much of this will be covered in greater detail in the chapter on "The Teacher in the Teaching Process".

Teaching should create a hunger in the student and a responsiveness that will actually bring about the results that the teacher is looking for. This seems to have been one of the gifts of Jesus in his teaching. He was able to create in the listener a hunger and thirst for righteousness and more of the Masters teaching. The aim or goal is a positive outcome, which is demonstrated in learned proficiency in the student. Laying a full and secure foundation sets the stage for future learning, and is the first concern for the professional educator.

*"Those that do teach young babes
Do it with gentle means and easy tasks;
He might have child me so; for, in good faith, I
am a child to chiding."
William Shakespeare, Othello ii 111*

*"Give me a child for the first seven years,
and he is mine forever"
A Proverb, Collins Dictionary of Quotes,
pg. 536, Harper Collins, 1995*

Chapter 5

Philosophy of Christian Education

Revelation

A Christian Philosophy of education begins with a theistic worldview. It by necessity begins with the reality of self-consciousness, as with most philosophical systems. Since the self is continuous and remains the same from experience to experience, awareness of that which is not of self becomes possible. Self-consciousness makes objectivity a possibility or reality. Humanity lives in a knowable world. The world can be discovered because we have the ability to be aware of other things around us besides ourselves. Thus, the kind of heart or perception a person has will determine the life that ultimately he will live.

A Christian worldview or a Christian philosophy of life commences with a Christian consciousness. This consciousness acknowledges the truth of God and humanities need for regeneration through Jesus Christ. A Christian philosophy will lead the honest searcher back to Christ. Thus, a Christian philosophy begins with an assumption. The assumption is that life and all worldviews leads to a conviction. As a Christian this conviction is that, *"God is, and He is a rewarder of those who diligently seek Him."*

A conviction that is strong and firm leads to confidence. This is equally true in terms of a basic understanding of who man is in relationship to God and His universe. This confidence leads to faith or reason. Faith and reason, from a Christian perspective, are compatible constructs. There are reasonable explanations to the way the universe is and reasonable understandings of who God is. Yet, ultimately God must be received, understood and experienced by faith. Thus, a Christian philosophy of education starts with God who is known through revelation. In figure 1 you will see an illustration of how this revelation is actually transmitted. It begins from the Godhead, the Trinity, the Father, Son and Holy Spirit, co-equal and co-existent. The Godhead is complete and totally God. He has provided for us special revelation through the Word of God. God's Word is inspired, having been written by the Holy Spirit over a fifteen hundred plus year period, through His chosen servants, and contains no contradictions in theme or purpose. God's Word is a special revelation that must be understood, read and studied as a part of a persons' faith in God.

Secondly, we have the general revelation of the existence of God and his purposes for mankind through creation. Creation itself can lead us to knowledge of a Supreme Being or of God. (Romans 1)

Finally, the most important and powerful personal and self-revelation was the coming of the incarnate one, the Lord Jesus Christ. Jesus coming to earth as man, taking on the form of man, is the ultimate expression of the revelation of God for all to see, know and experience. Thus, a Christian philosophy of education must begin simply with an understanding of who God is and how He has revealed Himself through history to mankind.

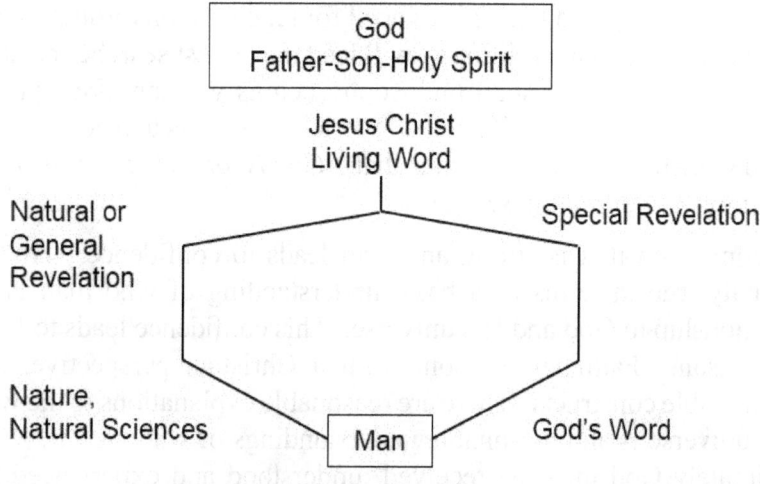

Figure 1

On Purpose

The purpose of God's revelation was to **make God known**. God revealed himself because God <u>wanted</u> to reveal himself. Therefore, God revealed himself. It is all a part of his decision. God is sovereign and he chose from the foundation of the world to reveal himself to his creation. The ultimate expression of that being the sending of his own dear Son.

The second purpose of God's revelation is **redemption**. God, in his grand foreknowledge, knew that man would sin with subsequent destruction upon God's wonderful creation. He planned from the beginning to send his Son to become the redeemer of the world. Prior to this revelation, the giving of the law, the life of faith in Abraham and the Davidic kingdom were all a part of God's revealed redemptive plan for mankind. This was culminated in the sending of Christ the Lord.

A Christian worldview begins with the revelation of God and it must be an unequivocal, firm belief system of every Christian educator. This belief leads to a central focus of teaching ministry, which is to transmit truth, reality, and the viability of this revelation to students.

Dr. H. W. Byrne, former Dean of Fort Wayne Bible College in Fort Wayne, Indiana, summarized for us a statement on a Christian theistic world view in his foundational book, "*A Christian Approach To Education.*" Briefly summarized here are his primary points as it pertains to this vital issue.

Our first point of reference begins with God. We believe that God is an eternal, personal being of absolute knowledge, power and goodness. He is ultimate reality and the source and ground of all reality and truth.

Christ the Son of God is creator, designer, and preserver of all things. In him the entire universe, macrocosm, microcosm, has its origin, energy, control and its final destiny. This relation between God and the world, organic and inorganic is expressed in such statements of scripture as Colossians 1:16,17 and Romans 11:36.

Man came into being by a direct immediate act of the creator. Unique among all creatures, he bears the image of God in that he has personality and the power of moral choice. He was created for a dual purpose. Godward, he is to glorify God and enjoy fellowship with him. Earthward, he is to subdue and hold dominion over the earth and its living creatures, (Genesis 1:28). Man's original state at creation has been changed by the intervention of sin. Through deliberate choice of the wrong, man has become estranged from God, the divine image has been marred and man is now morally corrupted and in need of redemption. God provides this redemption in the life, death, and resurrection of Jesus Christ. By faith in him as Savior and obedience to the Holy Spirit man may now be transformed unto God-likeness and restored to fellowship with God. Redemption includes the eternal destiny of man by receiving Christ as Savior, man is fitted for everlasting fellowship with God. Those who reject Christ are destined to everlasting separation from God. Redemption also assures that the earth which now suffers the effects of mans sin, shall be restored to its pristine perfection.

Truth like the created universe is centered in Christ (Colossians 2:3). It is therefore unity integrated by Jesus Christ in all of its parts, meaningfully related to each other and to Him. If truth originates in God, then He must communicate it to man. He does this by revelation. General revelation is the communication of truth through nature and providence. Special revelation includes a body of truth contained in the Bible and the disclosure of God and truth in the person of Jesus Christ. General revelation is in full harmony with special revelation and finds its true interpretation in it. The creator endows man with the power to apprehend truth. His senses lead to empirical truth, his reason gives him a grasp of more abstract forms of truth and faith, which is a positive response to God's revelation. This not only enables him by the Holy Spirit to understand the super rational, but also provides insight into the meaning of truth at all levels. Thus man can see things steadily; whole or completely.

As ultimate reality, God sets the standard by which value judgments are to be made. The highest good is realized in the exercise of his will and on the part of man in conformity to that will. Thus in light of a Christian worldview and as Christian educators, there are specific implications for the educational process. Simply put, the purpose then of education is to show God revealed. Our immediate objective of education is to qualify man to reveal God. Man must have a comprehensive viewpoint of understanding revelation and of transformation of individual lives physically, mentally, socially, morally and spiritually. That is, a transformation of his total environment or of the establishment of the kingdom of God here on earth. This leads to the need for quality curriculum, which has God as the central theme, presented as personal revelation through Christ, and by special revelation by God's Word.

Thus, any educational system within a local church, an adult education program, a children's church or Sunday school needs as a central focus a theistic worldview. That is, the overall philosophy of Christian education is the transmission of this theistic worldview. God is the center of all things as revealed to us ultimately through His Son Jesus Christ to our students. This is done for the benefit of the student, providing opportunity to receive that revelation and integrate it into all areas of their being.

"Where there is much desire to learn, there of necessity will be much arguing, much writing, many opinions; for opinion in good men is but knowledge in the making".

John Milton (1608-1674)
The Doctrine and Discipline of Divorce (1643)

Chapter 6

The Teacher In The Teaching Process

Herman Horne, author of *"The Master Teacher"* (published in 1942), made a very powerful statement in what he called the five essential qualities of a world class teacher. His essentials are worth repeating.

First of all, a world class teacher must have a worldview. He or she is not locked into just knowledge of his or her own individual world or subject matter. The broadened mind is able to bring a richness of experience to the educational process.

Secondly, a world class teacher has extensive knowledge of the subject matter that they teach. They are experts in their field, meaning they have placed a strong emphasis on their own academic training and development.

Third, they have a knowledge of their pupils. The pupil is the focus of the teaching ministry, making them quintessential to the process of imparted learning. It is vital to understand what the needs are of pupils in any given developmental stage. Thus, we can be more effective in our teaching methodology.

Fourth was an aptness to teach. A world class teacher has a gifting and aptitude for the communication of truth, knowledge, understanding, and wisdom. The master teacher enjoys the teaching process and has a gift of effective communication.

Finally, they have a character worthy of emulation. Not only are they excellent in their skill level in terms of the ability to communicate knowledge of their subject matter to the pupils, but, as individuals are positive role models within the adult community; someone that students can easily follow.

Teaching has been defined as the communication of experience from one person to another. Ultimately the teacher in teaching is one who is able to communicate their experience effectively, whether learned by their own educational process or from life. In this way, students will receive the knowledge, gain understanding and hopefully wisdom from the educative process.

While reflecting on the Master teacher, let us review some of the basic characteristics of a quality teacher, adding to what has been previously covered. This will include a review of the core characteristics of an accomplished instructor in terms of their life and skills within a classroom setting.

Core Characteristics

First of all, a good teacher is one that has genuine experience. Experience in the subject matter that is both real and applicable and can be shared in a clear and concise fashion to the student is required. A teacher must love their work and should have an enthusiasm for the work that they are called to. If they are delighting in the Lord as the scripture says, God will give them the desires of their heart (Psalm 37:4). One of the desires of the heart of a teacher is to impart knowledge and wisdom to the student. Thus, a teacher should delight in their subject. God can certainly help us to fall in love with the subject and communicate its worth as a natural part of life.

Another positive characteristic of a good teacher is that he/she has a continuous desire to learn. Their subject matter stimulates them. They have a hunger for their topic, which they transfer to their students. A teacher must continually search for greater knowledge that can be applied within the classroom. A good teacher is one that is not afraid to learn from their class experience, and use the class response as a barometer of the learning process.

Finally, a teacher should have a personal interest in their students. Students should have a confidence in them, which manifests as respect for the teacher. This respect is based upon speaking the truth in love with honesty and fairness. These attributes ultimately make students want to study. A teacher should have good personal self-discipline and be able to transfer that discipline to the students. This often takes patience, especially with those who struggle academically.

For another look at some of the key attributes of a good teacher, you might want to look into Appendix 1 under "10 Rules for Teachers."

Components of Educational Ministry

In his outstanding book, Models of Religious Education, Harold Burgess outlines six primary components of educational ministry. They include aim, content, teacher, learner, environment and evaluation. Each component is vital to the educational process.

Aim

The aim of instruction can be viewed differently according to content and preference. For Christian educators, a (if not the) primary aim or goal of instruction is the establishment or expansion of the kingdom of God. The Apostle Paul described the kingdom of God as more than daily experience (eating, drinking), but righteousness (right relationship with God and man) peace and joy, which comes from the Holy Spirit. In as much as the Holy Spirit has as primary function the revealing of truth to the believer, it can be rightly perceived that the educational process can and should be a cooperative ministry with the Holy Spirit to produce kingdom aims. The mere achieving of grades upon exams or the receipt of a diploma or degree is a far inferior aim.

Content

Christ is the ultimate content of instruction. To know him was Paul's highest desire and the transmission of the truth his consummate purpose. The student must be challenged to "see Jesus" in all his/her studies and experience Christ in daily life.

Regardless the discipline being presented, the foundational content of our instruction is Christ and His Word.

Teacher

Of course, the teacher is highly important in the instructional process. Even in independent study (not excluding the ever-present Holy Spirit), a teacher is perceived through textual material, video, online interaction or E-mail.

The teacher must be well prepared for the task given. Assuming proper preparation and heart attitude, most will instruct and impart with sufficient care to move the learner towards a Christ centered kingdom aim.

Learner

Not all students are learners. A learner is by definition one who has been or is being impacted by the instructional method (or by experience, illumination, etc.) and changing ever so slightly and profoundly because of this process. The learner must be willing to submit themselves to the learning process (have ears to hear and eyes to see) and commit themselves to complete the tasks assigned. Learning means much more than the memorization of facts (though this is an often neglected discipline) but includes the ability to assimilate, synthesize, evaluate and utilize information in daily experience.

To effectively learn, the student must have achieved sufficient maturation to process the information presented. Thus, the teacher should be well versed on the various stage theories and how they interact with the student in the learning environment. Key theories and theorists include Erik Erickson (Stages of Psychosocial Development), Piaget and his cognitive theories as related to learning readiness, Kohlberg and his moral development. The student must be capable of learning, and the task of a teacher is to adequately assess the level of ability to learn in the individual student.

Environment

The learning milieu may be varied, and is important in the educational process. It has been stated (by someone) that experience is the best teacher. That is probably only true if one learns from it. The milieu or environment created by the teacher can enhance or detract from the experience of education. Thus, it is important to order the environment to ensure the possibility of learning. Few benefits emerge from either extreme, absolute order or chaos. A controlled yet nurturing or accepting environment is far more desirable for the majority of learning tasks. However, competition with the latest high tech gadgets is not essential. Even in a less than desirable environment, a well prepared teacher and a hungering for righteousness learner can overcome any environmental difficulty.

Evaluation

Perhaps the most difficult aspect of teaching (and most certainly of being a student) is evaluation. Yet, evaluation of student progress in light of stated and preferably objective goals is essential to ensure not "missing the mark..." Whatever the learning task, some evaluation of the student and teacher is needed to make full the circle and to provide feedback for future educational endeavors.

The American society is rife with unaccountable mavericks, independent spirits who desire something for nothing. The price is too high. Proper evaluation allows for necessary remediation or adaptation necessary for future success, and is an essential component of educational ministry.

13 Points Of Light

What is a teacher like who is a prime mover in the teaching process? Listed here are thirteen points with some basic commentary, which hopefully will be instructive for the teacher and provide a view of the characteristics that an administrator should be looking for in a quality educator.

First of all, a teacher is one who will effect the eternity of others. I still remember my earliest experiences in kindergarten, even prior to that in Sunday School. My recollections are positive as my female teachers had a love for us as students. The feeling of being special in kindergarten, first and second grade classes, as well as in my Sunday School program was blissful. Often it was the elderly women, the grandmothers within the local church that were most influential and consistent overseers to my early education. In each case, their positive attitude and belief in my eternal destiny effected me. They were the pre-learning individuals or those that helped set the stage for my latter learning about the things of God. Their love led me to a personal relationship with Jesus Christ.

Secondly, a teacher is one who will assist another in the learning process. Their focus is not for their own gain and benefit, but is to assist the student to learn what is necessary during any given developmental period.

Thirdly, a teacher is one who imparts his knowledge to others. It's not the mere passing on of concepts and precepts to some unsuspecting young mind. A teacher is one who takes the knowledge that they have gained, synthesizes it for the individual student and transmits it through a communication process, both verbal and non-verbal, which will positively impact the individual student.

Fourth, a teacher is one who awakens another to the needs that they have in terms of both the learning process and in terms of their own growth and development. In the learning process, the teacher should motivate a child to want to learn, or as an adult instructor to do the same for the adult. Part of accomplishing this is to provide relevancy to the individual student while teaching with enthusiasm. The needs of the student should be impacted. Areas that need growth, development, change, and correction should be brought to the surface through the dynamics of interaction. Thus, through teaching alone, especially teaching of God's Word, character change will occur.

Fifth, a teacher is one who inspires others, both in the learning process in formal educational setting and in later life. Some of those motivators can be positive and negative. I still remember a teacher who gave me guidance when I was a senior in high school. My grade point average was at best average. She suggested that I consider finding a less academically challenging profession like working in the post office. In her opinion there was no way I would ever make it within a university. There was many a day when I wanted to send her a copy of my Ph.D., but by the time I got that far I no longer had the need.

Sixth, a teacher is one who guides others. To guide someone in the learning process is much more positive and powerful than forcing or manipulating him or her to learn. When a teacher leads someone into faith, the student discovers new things for themselves that creates an excitement of discovery, which is part of what motivates people to continue to learn.

Seventh, a teacher is one who brings correction, both in the grading of papers and in the discipline that sometimes needs to occur. A teacher brings correction to ensure a student understands where they stand in relationship to others, as well as what changes need to be made in order to successfully proceed in life. Any teacher that is afraid of hurting a student's feelings by not providing adequate feedback, in the long run, is hurting that student. An easy grade is too easy. A grade that is earned because of hard work brings about a positive sense of self worth, which is desperately needed for all students.

Number eight, the teacher is more important to the teaching-learning process than the method of teaching, the setting or even the tools that are used (such as visual aids, etc.). In other words, Jesus, as a master teacher, taught in a variety of settings, using a variety of methodologies (including the parabolic method, etc.). More important than any of those things was Jesus himself. He was what was being imparted, his character, his nature, his essence, was being revealed to his disciples through the educational methodology that he chose.

Christ' methodology was both example as well as didactic. He taught systematically. He sometimes used unusual settings and circumstances. Yet, in all cases, Jesus was involved in transmitting his life into his disciples, which is a part of what every instructor is tasked to do.

Ultimately great teachers are able to teach regardless of the setting or whether or not they have their educational "props." Administrators need to be aware of this reality since Christian educational settings often lack some of the materials that many of the public educational programs take for granted. Thus, it helps to have an ingenious teacher who is able to use "field fixes", able to figure out how to make things work as they go. Flexibility is a key.

Number nine, a teacher is a product of their own conscientious work towards excellence. A truly good teacher is one that has a positive pride in the work they accomplish. They have a desire and drive towards excellence. This characteristic is not easy to find, but when a teacher is willing to strive for excellence in their labor for the Lord, most of their students will tend to follow suit.

Number ten, a teacher is able to increase the abilities of the student by making the student aware of their own natural gifts and resources. It is said that all men are created equal. However not all are equal in terms of their gifts and abilities. For a teacher to take a borderline or intellectually challenged student and bring them to average might be a much more monumental task than keeping a highly capable and intellectual student on track. Just because someone is highly gifted and achieves "A's" does not mean that they are studying or doing their very best. A teacher will bring the best out of the student, whatever that is. In fact, in the book of Jeremiah the prophet proclaims a special blessing to those that are able to extract the precious from the worthless (see Jeremiah 15:19). In other words, when we are able to pull from inside an individual that which others might say has little or no merit, bringing it to the surface, allowing it to be seen and shine for the glory of God, demonstrates a master teacher in action.

Number eleven, a teacher can be seen as ninety percent of the overall curriculum. Textbooks are important, exams are vital, illustrations are necessary and visual aids a great help. Good teaching comes from good teachers. A teacher that is well prepared will be able to teach regardless of setting and will be able to make the curriculum come alive because it lives within them.

Number twelve, a teacher is a sculptor of souls. The soul is defined as the mind, the will and the emotions or the conscience of the person. Our task is to bring our pupils through the educational process into an encounter with the revelation of Jesus Christ found within God's Word. Thus, they will come to a place of choice. The choice being to obey God's Word, to take responsibility for their own life and move forward in their calling. In doing so we help the student to avoid projecting blame, becoming consummate victims and never achieving their destiny in the Lord. As a sculptor of souls we are not just increasing the intellectual capacity of the mind, we are also enhancing the control of the emotions and the ability to adequately and appropriately express them. We are also training the will to decide to do what is right in right situations based upon the principles of the Word of God.

Finally, a teacher is an ambassador of God here on earth. 2 Corinthians 5:20 says that we are ambassadors for Christ. As an ambassador, a teacher is one who represents God, communicating truths of the kingdom, representing the Lord to students. Thus, the Christian educator must be positive as a role model in every aspect of their life.

Section II

The Process Of Teaching

"He who can, does. He who cannot, teaches."
George Bernard Shaw (Education)

"For by this time you ought to be teachers, you have need again for someone to teach you the elementary principles of the oracles of God, and you have come to need milk and not solid food. For everyone who partakes only of milk is not accustomed to the word of righteousness, for he is a babe. But solid food is for the mature, who because of practice have their senses trained to discern good and evil.
Hebrews 5:12-14

Chapter 7

From The Heart and Head

So many people have tried to separate out the qualifications of a Christian teacher from that of other ministry positions within the Body of Christ. It is important to take a look at the two types of teachers presented within the scripture. Along with this, it is judicious to review the qualifications for each from a Biblical perspective in terms of the characteristics of first the heart, then the head. Two important points in regards to the heart should be remembered from the teaching of Jesus and Solomon. They said, *"out of the abundance of the heart the mouth speaks"* (Luke 6:45) and we must *"guard our hearts for out of it* (our heart) *flows the issues of life"* (Proverbs 4:23).

First, in Ephesians 4:10-11 the Word of God presents the five-fold ministry, one of which is the Teacher. A five-fold ministry teacher is a foundational ministry within the Body of Christ and is a gift to the Body given by Christ himself. These teachers provide foundational truth and are able to bring revelation of the knowledge of the Word of God in a way that is beyond a standard teachers' ability. In spite of the fact that they are especially gifted and anointed for the communication of the truth of God's Word, they still must meet the basic qualifications of elders as found within the Word of God. When Peter or Paul went to a city, even if they had ministered there before, they sat with the elders or joined them. Thus they were a part of that ruling presbytery or elder board and had to meet the qualifications of an elder in terms of their basic character. More on this gift to the church will follow.

The second gifting of teacher is found in Romans 12:3-18, NASB,

> *"For through the grace given to me, I say to every man among you not to think more highly of himself than he ought to think but to think so as to have sound judgment as*

> *God has allotted to each a measure of faith. For just as we have many members in one body and all the members do not have the same function so we who are many are one body in Christ and individually members one of another. Since we have gifts that differ according to the grace given to us let each exercise them accordingly. If prophecy, according to the proportion of his faith, if service in his serving, or he who **teaches in his teaching**, or he who exhorts in his exhortation, he who gives with liberality, he who leads with diligence, he who shows mercy with cheerfulness. Let love be without hypocrisy. Abhor what is evil, cling to what is good. Be devoted to one another in brotherly love, give preference to one another in honor no lagging behind. In diligence, fervent in spirit, serving the Lord, rejoicing in hope, persevering in tribulation, devoted to prayer, contributing to the needs of the saints, practicing hospitality. Bless those who persecute you, bless and curse not, rejoice with those that rejoice and weep with those who weep. Be of the same mind toward one another. Do not be haughty in mind but associate with the lowly. Do not be wise in your own estimation. Never pay back evil for evil to anyone. Respect what is right in the sight of all men and if possible so far as it depends on you, be at peace with all men."*

The Apostle Paul was espousing some poignant admonitions to leaders within the Body of Christ in Rome. In this one aspect, he is instructing teachers (teaching the teachers) to teach according to the portion of faith or the measure of faith that God has given them. Every teacher has an ability to teach at a certain level. Whatever that is, we are to teach to the best of our God given ability. Recognizing that we are but one part of the Body of Christ and thus are to be mutually submitted to one another. There are many other positive admonitions given by Paul in terms of how to treat one another in the Body of Christ, including blessing one another, praying for one another, rejoicing with one another, and not lifting oneself up higher than one should.

These are all to be part of the characteristics of a teacher. Thus, whether a five-fold ministry gifted teacher or one who is in the role of teaching children, young people or adults, it behooves all to teach to the best of their ability, while recognizing that God has called us all to have the mind of Christ. The mind of Christ is specifically spoken about in the book of Philippians 2:5-11, and says:

> *"Have this attitude in yourselves which was also in Christ Jesus who although he existed in the form of God did not regard equality with God a thing to be grasped but emptied himself taking the form of a bond-servant and being made in the likeness of men and being found in appearance as a man, he humbled himself by becoming obedient to the point of death even death on a cross. Therefore, also God highly exalted him and bestowed on him the name which is above every name that at the name of Jesus every knee should bow of those who are in heaven and on the earth and under the earth and that every tongue should confess that Jesus Christ is Lord to the glory of God the Father."*

The attitude of a teacher should be that of a humble servant of God and of one another. This attitude should be exhibited to those that appear to be "inferior" to the teacher within the classroom.

The Word of God places a much higher emphasis on character than charisma. This point has been well developed previously in this manuscript. It is important to remember that the heart of a leader or teacher that becomes divided or cluttered with the cares of their own life can cause great difficulty in the life of the student. It is encouraged as a teacher that if one is having difficulty dealing with feelings, hurts, or problems effecting their teaching ministry that they seek some outside consultation.

If ones' heart becomes embittered, resentful, angry, or filled with fear and anxiety, these wounds will ultimately be transmitted to the students. It is not possible to hide them forever. Thus, it is essential to deal with issues of our own heart, making certain that our eyes and heart are clear, so that effective communication of the truth of God and His Word to the students is possible.

From The Head

It certainly would be interesting to tap into the minds of any adult or child, listening in to their secret thought processes. One can only surmise what a child or young adult might be thinking at any given time. One thing is for certain, people are always thinking. Whether actively or passively, everyone is thinking all the time, and their thought are significant. When referring to the head, the focus is on what the teacher thinks about themselves and the educational process. What kind of mindset is required to be effective within the classroom setting?

As previously stated, a teacher must have a fully developed worldview and strong subject matter skills. Essentially, a teacher should have gone through a process of his or her own renewing of the mind. The teacher, administrator or whomever is functioning in the role of leader in Christian education must ensure that they have resolved much of their own personal conflicts. Thus, they are able to set aside, for the sake of the students, their own personal issues and agenda, prior to ministering to their intended audience. Certain issues in our minds must be clearly resolved before engaging our students. These include

Freedom And Authority

It is important to recognize that there must be a balance between freedom and authority. More on this will be discussed in detail in terms of the methodology of education and the techniques of teaching.

However, it is important to introduce this here. Every teacher needs to plan, in advance of their teaching a specific course, exactly how much freedom will be allowed in class. What is permissible, in terms of student interaction, classroom participation, the ability of the students to take liberties, movement about the classroom etc.

This freedom must be balanced by how much authority and/or structure is to be provided by the teacher in order to facilitate the educational process.

Teachers are authority figures. This authority is provided to the educator through the parents and ultimately extends from God himself. Educators do have inherent in the position or role as an educator, the ability to stand in the position of loco parentis or in the place of the parents. Thus, the source and authority for a Christian educator comes from God through the parents. Exactly how this authority is exercised and how one deals with problems of discipline within the classroom must be thought through well in the advance of the start of class. Every teacher needs to spend time inside of their own head, thinking through how to present the educational material and how to function as a parental figure in terms of both communicating the material as well as disciplining students when they misbehave.

Generally speaking, the more structured a teacher is, the more secure the class will feel. The more secure the class feels, the better they will perform and the less the need to act out or act up to determine the level of authority a teacher may or may not have. Thus, the process of classroom planning is a cognitive exercise of great importance.

> *"LEARN TO WRITE WELL,
> OR NOT TO WRITE AT ALL."*
>
> *JOHN SHEFFIELD,
> ESSAY ON SATIRE, 1.281*

Chapter 8

The Curriculum

In Byrne's book "A Christian Approach to Education: A Bibliocentric View" previously referred to, the author provides a definition of the term Christian curriculum. Byrne states, "the word Christian will determine the answer. Education is distinctively Christian when the authority of Christ and the realization of his authority in our lives is the justification for all educational activity. The subject matter will be recognized as a revelation of his truth. All activities will be motivated by his life, will and spirit. Whether conceived in broad or narrow terms, a Christian curriculum centers in Christ. It is the medium employed by the school to achieve the ends of Christian Education." (Pg. 151)

A curriculum is the design of a course of study. There are various ways to organize a curriculum to ensure that the learning process will be conducted in a positive and progressive manner. There are four major theories or constructs of which can be applied to various fields of study. They include:

1. The information or knowledge concept.
2. The disciplinary concept.
3. The social concept.
4. The creative concept.

Each offers a unique perspective on the educational ministry.

First, is the knowledge concept of the curriculum. In this concept, the primary purpose of the curriculum is to enhance the students' ability to master certain subject matter from an intellectual vantagepoint. In other words, learning is measured by the amount of information a student is able to memorize and retain over time.

In certain courses, especially math or science, memorization is an essential part of learning. However, in the modern age of information retrieval, it is less likely that a student must memorize long lists of facts and figures to function adequately in society.

Secondly is the disciplinary concept. In this concept, the process of how the student learns becomes more important than what they learn. The goal is to assist the student to increase their mental capacities and powers of reasoning and maximize the students' problem solving capabilities, which are obviously desirable skills for life. Christian educators are most acutely interested in a students' ability to assimilate information or data, along with their skill in applying new knowledge to real life scenario. Educators hope students will learn to synthesize information, and thus learn to think in real world terms from a Christian mindset.

The third concept is the social, which stresses the noble desire that every student function as an exemplary citizen within culture. For the Greeks, learning was to lead to sterling character, and this prime educational goal has been inherited (unfortunately lost to many) by the Western world. That is, the teachings and philosophy was designed to make one an effective and well-informed citizen of Greek society. This same goal is the hope of many present day educators, both secular and Christian. The goal is to assist individuals to function adequately within a civilized social structure. In the emerging international or inter-cultural world, we live in, having a Christian world view that is also transmittable into a variety of cultural settings should be a goal of the educational curriculum from a social concept model.

The fourth is the creative concept, which places added emphasis on the individual pupils' ability to be creative in the learning process. Learning activities are arranged to motivate the power of self-expression, self-appraisal and self-activity. In other words, to learn the joy of an internalized self-motivation for learning. The curriculum thus consists of activities that are adjusted constantly to fit changing student needs.

Each of the above concepts contains elements which are desirable in teaching students. How does a Christian educator view these basic concepts of curriculum development in light of present instructional methods?

Individual educators are interested (or at least should be) in the whole man. The prime objective of education is the growth and development of each child or adult, assisting them to become fully what God intended them to be. One scripture which speaks to the process and importance of a growth motif is found in Luke 2:52. Here we can see a brief picture of the educational life of Jesus. It states,

> *". . . and Jesus kept increasing in wisdom and stature and in favor with God and men."*

He grew spiritually, in terms of the grace of God; socially in terms of the grace or favor of men; physically in terms of his stature and in wisdom, in his intellectual life or mental activities. A philosophy of Christian education should include a holistic viewpoint of students, showing care and concern for each area of growth stated here.

Secondly, as students are taught, an emphasis on character change, assisting the individual to become conformed to God's image is paramount. The fact is, sin has tainted every aspect of human existence. Thus, a soteriological emphasis or redemptive focus in educational programs that are developed is wise.

There is much to be commended in the social concept of curriculum development. To recognize that mankind has a responsibility to society as well as to one another is commendable. The Word of God highly esteems covenant relationship with God and with one another. Thus, learning cooperative relationships and proper social interaction is important. Further, most Christians would agree in principle with the creative concept of curriculum development. The importance of the child and their unique nature should be considered when teaching. However, we must be careful to have a clear understanding of the self-actualization process. A humanistic form of self-actualization leads the student away from a trust in or dependency on God. True self-actualization should bring a person to the recognition of God's preeminence in life. It is only in Him that, *"we live and more and have our being"* (Acts 17:28).

Once an educator has determined what the overall curriculum should be in terms of philosophical approach, and the type of learning activities to develop, then the actual content of the curriculum is to be developed. In Christian schools as with most Sunday School programs, curriculum is usually pre-developed. Most of the curriculum is subject related and the content is primarily developmental in approach. Its design is based upon standardized learning principles and the respective needs of children and adults. Thus, a teacher uses materials to teach from that fit with the developmental age and capabilities of the "average" child, whatever that may be.

What is being suggested here is that the Christian educator should teach curriculum, whether self-developed or provided, with an integrative approach in mind. Even if teaching English, math, science or theology, it must be taught with specific aim, objective or purpose in mind. Each of the concepts presented above should be considered in reviewing and utilizing a curriculum. It must be viewed in light of the educational needs of the students, while being mindful of a Christian worldview. A teacher may then impart knowledge and truth, facts and figures, concerns of social content and creativity that will necessarily assist the student to learn fully the material presented in a given course or study. In developing curriculum, it is essential to think through the goals of the class. Care must be taken to ensure that all of the materials used will work together in the attainment of the goals of the course.

Finally, again in Byrne's text *"A Christian Approach to Education,"* he lists, quoting Professor Nelson Bossing of the University of Minnesota, a series of steps to be followed in curriculum construction. They have been listed here with brief commentary.

Step one is to have a clearly defined conception of the curriculum. That is, what is the subject that is intended to be taught and why is it important to that individual student.

Step two would be a statement of a social educational philosophy. Most of this has been covered in earlier sections of this book but it should be reiterated in the development of the purpose statement for your curriculum. That is, the basic Christian worldview should be strongly emphasized.

Step three is a statement of the basic principles of learning accepted. What learning is to take place within the course? What things are considered requirements of a student that has taken a course in English, literature or math in terms of end results?

Step four is a statement of the aims of education. What does the teacher intend to accomplish and how does he or she intend to do it?

Step five covers scope, areas of curriculum and course of study. What is to be studied and what will not be studied? What is within the scope or the parameters of this course? In certain subjects, such as history, there is tremendous diversity of content and many ways that the course can be approached. Therefore, we must set clear boundaries on the curriculum. To have too wide a scope might make it too expansive for many students. Further, the scope of instruction must be kept within the context of the individual students' social and intellectual capabilities. This takes discipline of thought and intention.

Step six is sequence and time allotment. As the teacher prepares the curriculum, how much time and in what order will the teaching of the material be presented? The Bible speaks about doing things line upon line, precept upon precept, here a little, there a little (see Isaiah 28:10).

A similar learning principle, taken from the Word of God, is taking someone from *"glory to glory,"* (see 2 Corinthians 3:18).

This can also be illuminated in the meaning of the Greek word for salvation (*sozo*). A literal meaning of this word is *wholeness* or *completeness*. Salvation happens at the moment that one is born again (see John 3:6, John 1:12-13), and continues as a process of sanctification (see Philippians 1:6). So, one is saved, is being saved and will be saved. One is justified, in the process of being sanctified and ultimately will be glorified. The Christian walk is a continually increasing or transforming growth process. Each stage is built upon previous ones, until we come to the full measure of Christ (see Ephesians 4:13, Hebrews 6:1).

We can see from scripture that there is by design (God's) a sequencing to learning, growth or change. Thus, teaching must be mindful of this reality, and must be kept within standard time allotments, if healthy and fruitful progress is to be made. One of the true gifts and art forms of education is making sure that the curriculum is adequately taught within the time allowed.

Step seven is a determination of the content materials and activities. What educational material and activities will be necessary to communicate the content of the course material? Is a lecture method adequate to present the material professionally and fully, or will other activities and materials be necessary? Will illustrations be used, etc.? A decision on materials to be used for content delivery must be made.

Step eight is the organization of materials and activities. Once the content of materials has been made, they must be organized properly. Much of this will be covered in the next section on "The Methodology of Teaching."

Step nine is the teaching procedures. How will the content of the course be taught?

Step ten is the evaluation of the procedure. How will the instructional process, to include the evaluation of the student be covered? How will the teaching methods be evaluated?

Step eleven is the pupil/teacher reference materials. What materials in addition to the actual teaching are required as resources or reference materials for the student? This can be as simple as referring them to their library.

Step twelve is the mechanical make-up of the course of study. What is the logistics of the classroom setting; how does the teacher intend to develop the educational curriculum? What will the end results be should the course follow the plan committed to?

In light of these suggestions, many groups have developed uniform procedures and processes for curriculum development. Some of the typical processes found include:

1. The formulation of course of study outlines from the Bible.
2. The editorial process which details the planning of materials, which includes quality, costs, number of materials needed, etc. Further, it will require;
   a. The selection of who will write the curriculum.
   b. A conference with those writers for coordination purposes.
   c. Policies regarding the use of copy righted materials.
   d. Writing the actual curriculum units or courses.
   e. The review of the manuscripts.
   f. Revision of manuscripts,
   g. experimentation with materials,
   h. editing for accuracy,
   i. lay-out printing and eventually audio/visual additions or other materials necessary.

Thus, there is a long and detailed process that goes into the developing of a quality curriculum.

In reality, there is nothing new under the sun. Much of the materials that a teacher will find developed are an adaptation of previous materials. Just as many books are written based upon what has already gone before them, just worded or developed in a slightly different way that hopefully will add new truth to the existing volume of written material, so it is with curriculum development. I strongly encourage that the student and administrator of Christian educational programs become well versed with a variety of curriculums devised and developed for Christian education. The more that we know about various curriculum, the more the educator can effectively choose curriculum that will accomplish the purpose of teaching and blessing the student.

"There is no such whetstone, to sharpen a good wit and encourage a will to learn, as is praise."
Roger Aschain (1515-1568)

"Let such teach others who themselves excel, and censure freely who have written well."
An essay on Criticism, 1711, line 15,
Alexander Pope (1688-1744)

Chapter 9

The Methodology

The methods of teaching can vary greatly depending upon the individual philosophy of the educational system and/or educator.

A primary purpose or methodology in secular education is to vary the environment of the pupil with the hope that this modification will bring about a change in the students' mind and personality. This method will bring about some positive, favorable results, though it is somewhat of a mechanical viewpoint of the teacher-student process. There are other varying methodologies used throughout history, which may lend insight into modern methodologies.

The first and the most revered by many is the Socratic method. Its name comes from the Greek philosopher Socrates who lived in the 5th century B.C. His methodology employed the primary usage of questions and answers. He did not approach the educational setting with pre-determined answers, but assumed that answers to various questions would come through the interactional process. Even when Socrates gave answers himself, he rarely did so directly. He usually put them in the form of questions. Thus, he became a learner along with the pupil. Later this style of education became known as a dialectic method of education.

Throughout the Middle Ages the primary method of teaching was imitation and memory. That is, the students spent most of their time reproducing materials that had been given to the student by the teacher. This technique, practiced most often in some Christian Educational systems seems a bit boring at best but is probably somewhat effective in terms of the transmitting of information from one generation to the next.

The lecture method arose out of the primary customs of professors in the medieval universities. These professors had a prime motivation of providing the most information in the least amount of time. This was necessary due to the scarcity of books and other resource material. Thus, the students took copious notes of the lectures given by the instructors as a way to develop their own library. This method is still used quite exclusively in many Two-thirds World nations for the same reasons as in medieval times.

This method continued until Erasmum, who tied subject matter together with the natural interest of the pupil. Thus began the process of developing the first form of curriculum or of developing courses based upon the needs of students. His approach was a bit more informal and cooperative.

In the sixteen and seventeen centuries, harsh discipline was used to ensure that the educational processes were completed. Frequently, severe punishment was used upon students to ensure that they would stay on task and learn the assigned material. The emphasis was on how to learn more than what was actually learned. John Locke was a primary advocate of this methodology.

More modern methods of education began with Comenius (1592-1670). He advocated methods of education that appealed to the five senses. He promoted the use of pictures, object lessons and other forms of education that would ensure that the primary modalities of sensory input were all touched by the teaching methods.

Rousseau (1712-1778) continued and expanded on the methodology of Comenius. Yet, he also insisted that education was more a process of doing than of knowing. He included feeling in his methodology, developing a certain romantic element to his method of teaching.

Ultimately, Comenius emphasized the physical senses and Rousseau an individual's native tendency. Pestalozzi (1746-1827) was able to demonstrate how a teacher can use these concepts in classroom instruction. "He stressed pupil activity through the use of object lessons and physical objects as the best way to learn and teach" (pg. 181 of Byrne's book). Therefore, the pupil was able to learn from first hand experience. The student was no longer to be a passive observer but a full participant in their own education.

Ultimately, it was Herbart (1776-1841) who placed the greatest emphasis on various steps that educators could take to assist the students to a complete learning experience. According to Herbart, there are five distinct steps that a teacher could follow to be highly effective. They were:

- The first step was **preparation.** The teacher will begin a class with a preliminary overview or will present material that will set the stage for later learning.
- The second step is **presentation.** Present any new materials that are to be learned by the student.
- The third step is **association.** This involves a comparison on the part of the pupil of the materials in the first two steps. Thus, when the individual student is able to see a relationship between former learning and new learning, then the assimilation of that new material becomes possible.
- The fourth step involves **systemization** or the general classification of knowledge into categories. The teacher provides for the class several examples of the material being taught so it can be applied to other areas of the students' lives. This has a lot to do with the concept of **relevancy**.
- The fifth and final step is **application.** Application involves assignments that the individual can do to practice what they have learned up to that point.

This overall methodology remains prevalent today, although other educators such as Horace Mann, Froebel and others have modified it to a certain extent.

In the modern era, other teaching methodologies have come to the forefront. John Dewey, considered the father of modern education, developed his problem method. Dewey advocated learning by doing. His "doing" was towards a specific and measurable end, not merely busy work. Consequences and outcomes of study were important to Dewey. An emphasis on the completion of projects was also introduced by William Kilpatrick and can be seen in many modern educational programs today.

A Christian Application

As Christians our concept or method should be somewhat different than that of the secular community. First of all, and of great importance, we teach from a different philosophical ground, discussed earlier as our theistic worldview. This states that God revealed all truth through either general revelation in nature, special revelation in scriptures, or through personal revelation through Jesus Christ. This leads the professional Christian educator to a belief in objective reality flowing from an objective revelation of God, which is knowable and to be presented within a classroom structure. Thus, in terms of a Christian approach to methodology, it rightly parallels a Christian understanding of truth. There are four possible approaches to truth. One is revelation alone. Two is revelation plus reason. Three is reason alone. Fourth is revelation plus reason plus experimentation. Where revelation is used alone, the danger of suppressing our ability to reason can lead to irrational belief systems. Reason must supplement our revelation. Revelation plus reason in and of itself is not fully adequate in explaining all that one can discover. Thus, ultimately experimentation can lead to deeper understanding of truth that one can find in nature and in relationship with one another.

Probably the most accepted form of teaching methodology today is the inductive/deductive method. By inductive, what is meant is that the learner is able to gather information and knowledge from the study and examination of facts in an attempt to determine various principles. By deduction, what is meant is that there are certain principles that are inherent within scientific methodology. Thus one is able to evaluate facts on the basis of those principles. Both are required in tandem to correct the thinking process.

To further look at an inductive method in terms of the study of the scriptures, scripture must be observed, classified and analyzed to be understood. Conclusions are then drawn from these particulars.

This method is therefore relatively inductive because pure induction is rare if not virtually impossible. It demands first hand observation, interpretation, evaluation, application and correlation of the material being learned. So inductive teaching is dependent upon forms of inductive study done by the individual student. A skillful teacher can use questions, lay out various materials and allow the students inductively to determine what the meaning, purpose or the usage of a certain curriculum is, and what the "correct" answers are to a given problem being studied.

In terms of the deductive method there are certain principles of learning and problem solving that (generally speaking) are known primarily by the teacher and thus must be presented to the student so that those principles can then be applied in a more inductive fashion. Thus, a teachers' methodology can flow back and forth between an inductive and deductive format, which seems to be the most effective method of instruction.

Of course, there are reactions to this more objective and rational method of education. Legitimate criticism comes from the adult education community that emphasizes the prophetic or the revelational aspects of knowing truth. Many would emphasis a transformational curriculum. (see Virkler, Mark, "Teaching For Transformation"[8] Communion With God Press). That is, a curriculum that is primarily designed to transform individuals thinking from a more spiritual dynamic dimension. They advocate a pure revelational or inspirational model. That is, if an individual is properly in tune with the Holy Spirit, able to pray effectively, God will personally reveal to them all they need to know to live life to its fullest. The goal of this method of instruction is for the student to become his or her own teacher, with assistance of the Holy Spirit, providing all necessary instruction throughout this intuitive/ revelational model.

---

[8] This is by necessity a simplistic view of Dr. Virkler's teaching program. It certainly deserves a more thorough review, but is beyond the scope of this study.

This method is reactionary from the purely objective processes frequently observed in the more traditional (sterile) Bible colleges and theological seminaries. A combination of both methods is the most powerful. Recognizing God's continuing ability to reveal himself in very personal ways remains possible and essential. The Holy Spirit desires to bring life into whatever curriculum is presented. Yet the tools of discovery (hermeneutics, exegesis, general research methods) remain vital to ensure orthodoxy and proper balance.

More on "Revelational Model"

In Charismatic circles this revelational model is often called "the anointing," or the unction of the Holy Spirit. This anointing brings life to the educational program, and a sense of excitement to the learning process. Without the anointing, without inspiration, without the breathing of the Holy Spirit (inspiration) upon a book, article or teaching setting, it becomes simply objective, often times perceived as irrelevant to the student. Thus, in terms of overall methodology, both heart and mind are essential. Both spirit and science are required. Educators need to be open, not to the irrational, but to the inspirational move of God's Spirit as curriculum is being taught within a classroom setting, while utilizing solid biblical study methods.

The Techniques of Teaching

Teaching is both a science and an art form. It has been the attempt to integrate these concepts as a conscious effort. In Christian education the hope is to assist students to learn whatever it is that is being taught, for the benefit of the student and society as a whole. In essence, this presents the teacher with a four-fold task.

Inspiration

1. A teacher must be able to enthusiastically inspire a student to want to learn whatever it is that is being taught. In my opinion, this is the most important and often the most

difficult task a teacher faces. In terms of teaching techniques, the teacher is to a great extent the technique. Having a sense of humor, being able to provide various and sundry experiences (personal stories of relevance), the ability to build relationships with students, all are a part of the requirements to inspire a student to learn. A teachers own level of intensity or desire toward the subject matter being taught can make the educational process much more fulfilling.

Impartation

2. The teacher is called upon to instruct the student, imparting information to produce understanding leading to wisdom. Information alone will produce little change of heart or mind, but must be combined with knowledge experienced, understood by the student, and if applied to life indicates wisdom gained. This is a difficult but worthy goal of education.

Discipline and Control

3. The teacher must effectively discipline the student. Teacher control or classroom management is necessary for instruction to pursue. I have seen many teachers who have excellent knowledge of their subject matter, good overall communication skills, a heart of love and compassion for their students, but who are ineffective as teachers. This is often caused by an inability to bring control or authority (which is required for the learning process) to the classroom. Thus, they become totally frustrated in their role and may experience burn out. It is tragic to when this occurs, but it often will. Professional teachers' are responsible to apply adequate classroom disciple, exercising it judiciously, ensuring that the teaching or learning environment is conducive for student growth. Christian educators must learn the art of speaking the truth

in love, acting in kindness, while firmly applying classroom management techniques for proper control and stability.

Achievement

4. The teacher must evaluate student achievement. It is best to do so from an honest and objective vantage point. We must honestly admit that objectivity is at times difficult. Little things that students do positively or negatively can easily influence our evaluation of them. For instance, while in 6th grade, penmanship was highly touted. Unfortunately, my fine motor skills were less than desirable. To compensate for my writing like a doctor before my time, I practiced perfect penmanship on a notepad, placing it on my teacher's desk for her to see. The writing done exclaimed how grateful I was for her teaching me (a little manipulative I know!). When the grading period came, though I continued to write as always, the grade given was a B+, much higher than deserved though gratefully appreciated. Thus, there is limited validity to the concept of total objectivity or being unbiased in the evaluation process. However, we must attempt to the best of our ability to remove personal bias, keeping prejudice in check.

Preparation, Presentation and Evaluation

Thus, the teaching process can be seen as embodied in three primary stages: the preparation for teaching, the presentation of teaching and the evaluation of the teaching process.

Preparation means simply that a teacher must do his or her own personal study. A teacher must have mastered the lesson before attempting to teach it. It is helpful to master the entire curriculum prior to teaching, but in reality, many times the best one can hope for is to stay a step or two ahead of the students. Thus, plan a lesson in advance and then present that lesson in such a way that it will build one lesson upon the other. This is the goal of preparation.

In terms of **presentation** in teaching, this is where the art form comes in. Asking yourself some key questions might help, as will keeping a focus within the context of the four primary areas of development as found in Luke 2:52. In other words, what is it that the students need to know? What goals are to be accomplished? How would I like my students to feel as they learn the subject matter? Would I like them to be excited, to feel passion, compassion, or sadness? What emotional need will I touch through my teaching? What is it that I would like for my students to do with the material that is being presented, besides just put the notes into a file folder and eventually regurgitate it on an examination? Ultimately, what kind of individual am I trying to produce, and how will this lesson move them in that direction?

Also, it is helpful to think of the specific time frame in which the materials are to be presented.

One helpful concept can be to view teaching in a three segment or stage process. This is similar to what counselors do in approaching a client. That is, begin by telling the client what you are going to be telling them. Then, you tell them what you intended to tell them. Finally, you tell them what you told them. This is also how many preachers will describe their preaching methodology or homiletic style. This is overly simple but filled with truth.

In the lesson plan for the teaching time, begin with a summary of what has been taught thus far, then introduce the next lesson. You might state, "What we are going to be studying today is. . ." with a focus on increasing their overall interest in the subject by linking it to the most recently reviewed materials.

As a positive professional teacher, it is helpful to wet their appetite or increase their enthusiasm and excitement about what is to come. There are many different methods for accomplishing this and we must find our own style and begin to use it. Sometimes observing master teachers will help. Some teachers will start with a story.

Some will start with an illustration. Some jump right into the lesson and, because of their own natural enthusiasm, the students grab on to the teaching and attend with delight (or at least passive tolerance).

Telling the students what you are telling them is to present the actual meat of the lesson for that day. Again, using the counseling field for an example, what most counselors begin a counseling session with is a review of how the week has been, briefly covering where they have been since the beginning of the counseling process. The meat of the counseling for that session will begin by simply asking, "What is it that will be covered now?" In counseling, the process is typically more inductive than deductive. But it can be deductive in that the counselor may set the agenda for discussion. Thus the counselor may state "today we need to be discussing the following." Then the process begins.

Then, near the end of the class, somewhere around ten minutes before the class time is over, there needs to be a review. The teacher will tell the students again what they have just been told. A summary of the inductive learning process is given. When this is completed, it brings closure to the classroom time. The goal is to leave room for questions and answers as a natural part of the educational program, so the teacher needs to plan for classroom participation.

Teaching proceeds from one time segment to another. Often educators are required to teach several different topics to the same students. This may entail communicating with several different age groups or varying populations and intellectual capabilities. In each situation there needs to be adequate time in preparation, to carefully evaluate methodology for the presentation of the material for maximum benefit.

Illustration

In a trip to Africa, I had an opportunity to have a conversation with one of the primary co-ministers working with Rinehart Bonke's evangelistic ministry. She shared with me that this great evangelist, who has won hundreds of thousands, even millions of people to

Christ, has five primary messages he will preach on any given crusade night. Yet, before each time he preaches, he spends time alone in his hotel room or wherever he can gather himself to seek the Lord intently, asking, "What should I preach tonight?" You would think after all these years it would be so easy for him to make this decision. But he wants to make sure that whatever it is that he is going to preach will be done according to the perfect will of the Father. He is determined to be personally, spiritually, and mentally prepared.

Weimers Big 5

In Mary Ellen Weimer's book, "Improving Your Classroom Teaching," she states that there are five primary components of effective instruction. They include <u>enthusiasm</u>, <u>preparation</u> and <u>organization</u>, ability to <u>stimulate student thought</u> and <u>interest</u>, <u>clarity</u> and <u>knowledge,</u> and <u>love of</u> the <u>content</u>. Let's look at these in some detail.

Enthusiasm

Enthusiasm speaks of a zest for teaching. Being enthusiastic is not easy for many teachers. Some, who by nature are more melancholy of temperament, are less excitable as individuals. However, regardless of natural tendencies, enthusiasm can be mustered, as it is a most important component of quality teaching. Weimer lists some very important points to ponder regarding enthusiasm and how it relates to educational ministry. First she suggests that we "<u>try not to be enthusiastic</u>." This sounds like a contradiction, but it's not. Students can perceive very quickly whether or not a teacher is faking their enthusiasm. That is, if a teacher attempts to be over the top in their enthusiasm about a course, masking either their insecurity or the lack of genuine enthusiasm, it will be quickly discovered. The teacher must find in the subject matter and/or their calling reason to be enthusiastic, and do so in their own natural way.

Also, she recommends that we take a brave and adventurous risk. That is, do the very best to be as enthusiastic about the subject matter as possible. We should teach in such a way that it will be exciting for the student. One problem that may mask positive enthusiasm is a heightened state of nervousness or anxiety. Thus, we must learn to control nervousness and work toward cultivating and maintaining confident enthusiasm. Enthusiasm should be easy for a Christian teacher if they recognize the tremendous responsibility and the wonderful opportunity that God has given them to participate in this outstanding area of ministry.

Preparation and Organization

The second principles according to Weimer are <u>preparation</u> and <u>organization</u>. This means more than syllabi development. It includes the ability to identify the objectives for a class and/or student and determine what the overall course content will be so effective communication of truth occurs. We must develop and design learning activities that will enhance the learning process. Objectives need to be geared to the level or capability of the student. We might ask ourselves what are the key questions that should be answered by the students as they commence their course of study? What information is critical and must be clearly imparted? How should this be accomplished? Our preparation needs to be strategized prior to the teaching of the course.

Included in preparation would be the classroom policies and procedures. That is, how will grading, attendance, academic integrity, the asking of questions, the overall flow of the class be negotiated? Again, each instructor is different and must find their own way of doing this properly. It is also important, in terms of overall organization and preparation to determine policies regarding absenteeism. If students are not in class, it will be most difficult for them to learn.

Most teachers develop fairly extensive outlines of their topic prior to teaching. In fact, they often prepare significantly more material than can be covered within the course time frame. The ability to plan efficiently comes through trial and error. The teacher should work to modify outlines, or think in terms of providing additional outlined notes to students that will supplement the classroom experience. In terms of teaching methodology, most teachers need to develop an outline, which will also sequence time, so that we can properly cover the material in a comprehensive fashion. This is by far one of the most difficult tasks for teachers, especially for new ones.

Thought and Interest

This third principle is stimulating student <u>thought</u> and <u>interest</u>. It is our consummate hope to create a desire within the student to learn what is taught and stimulate their intellectual growth. Good teaching will create questions in the student. Thus, our teaching methodology should encourage and give time for the students to develop questions and ask them. A bombastic educator, dogmatically authoritative in style, may intimidate students into passive acceptance of all being taught. This merely creates dependence on the teacher to answer all questions and do the thinking for the student. This is hardly the goal. Part of the art of eliciting questions is setting an environment where the student feels safe to inquire. In many academic settings a question is viewed as a challenge for the professor or teacher and subsequent dialog (if any) becomes nothing more than a "one-upsmanship" game. The students speedily learn that a question is not a question, a question is the opening round of an often brutal contest. Both the student and the professor, for sake of ego, must win. A way of encouraging interaction is to establish an environment where stimulating thought and discussion can occur.

In light of this it is helpful to ensure that discussion is led, not stampeded. That is, allow for a certain amount of interaction without allowing it to run amuck. Secondly, it is helpful to encourage group participation, small group interaction amongst the students, even making this one of the assignments of the class. This encourages maximum participation in the course material, and will increase problem-solving skills for the students.

Clarity

The fourth principle is <u>clarity</u> or the ability to explain things in a clear and effective manner. To describe someone that is clear in his or her teaching method is relatively simple. A skilled instructor has the ability to understand when students are confused or unable to follow a certain point, and will with skill and sensitivity eradicate the confusion, thus enlarging their ability to understand. This can be accomplished in a number of ways, including presenting alternative explanations or utilizing illustrations that will clarify. Sometimes it is the ability to take an idea, break it down into smaller bits, and then reintegrate it as a whole picture which makes instruction easier to follow and understand. Truly gifted instructors are able to make things relevant to the student.

In order to teach clearly and in a concise manner, a teacher must be able to understand what information the students are learning and how they are actually processing the material presented. It behooves the teacher to cogently observe students for their reactions, periodically asking for feedback as to the students' level of comprehension. Insuring understanding is risky but rewarding. Teachers seeking clarity take the responsibility to communicate in a succinct manner.

Most teachers have invested tremendous time learning their subject matter well. Thus, it can be easy to assume that since we are familiar with the language structure of a particular discipline that the students will be as well. This is a seriously flawed assumption. It is essential to clarify our known constructs, by providing clear definitions for the various words and principles taught. The most effective way to do so is to have definitions already prepared, written out before class begins. The teacher can provide the definitions to the students, making them responsible for grasping and remembering the meanings of key words and principles.

Even then, a teacher will need to spend time and energy clarifying difficult concepts, to ensure that what the student has read is crystal clear in their minds. Clarity is essential for learning; understanding what is taught in the way that it was meant to be received is the goal.

Relevancy can also be developed through using various examples and illustrations that students will directly relate to. The age or the developmental level of the students along with the type of class being taught will determine what kinds of illustrations will be best. For example, primary age children can learn best by hands on illustrations. Bringing a rabbit to class to illustrate how loving care for another could be an appropriate illustration. In preaching, an illustrated sermon, where the pastor or helper "acts out" a potion of the message can bring the teaching home. It is said that a picture is worth a thousand words. This is only true if the picture is clear and concise, appropriate to the age of the learner, and effectively presented.

A primary challenge for teachers is ensuring that every student in a classroom is able to understand the dynamic teaching being presented. This is an ideal that we work toward in everything that we teach. This is particularly true in light of the lofty goals as Christian educators. Where there is a lack of understanding, there is an inability to be obedient to what is being taught.

Of course, one difficulty faced by all educators, especially in terms of biblical teaching, is what the Bible calls hard-heartedness, or being stiff-necked. To soften the heart of students is a goal of the teacher, and requires a creative flare (not even signs, wonders and miracles can do it for some students).

Unfortunately, there are some students who are hard-hearted (or perhaps, hardheaded is more accurate) and will not open themselves up to learning. This being the case, the best we can hope for is that at least some seed of our teaching will get through the cracks in the students' armor, eventually producing good fruit in season.

Knowledge And Love

The fifth principle is <u>knowledge</u> and the <u>love</u> of your own <u>content</u>. Again, in Weimer's book she makes a rather important statement about various assumptions that need to be reevaluated. They include:

- **Assumption #1:** More is always better when it comes to the amount of content in a course. Its corollary assumption is that covering content equals teaching. It ain't necessarily so!
- **Assumption #2:** The most appropriate instructional orientation of a faculty is to the content, witnessed by the statement, I teach chemistry, political science, health education, biblical studies or whatever, not "I teach students."
- **Assumption #3** If you know it you can teach it.

Each of these assumptions is worth evaluating. Often, more is not better. Especially when realizing the limited attention span of both children and adults. It is more important to sequence teaching so that the student has the ability to comprehend small bits of the material than to attempt to put too much into the teaching time. This is one danger inherent in preaching and in teaching seminars. Putting a very large amount of content reduced into a smaller period of time can thoroughly overload the students. Therefore, an instructor must only attempt to teach as much as a student can reasonably comprehend.

Further, it is a terrible misnomer to think that we are teachers of a certain subject matter. An educators goal is to teach students. That's why the Christian philosophy of education, which is to produce a balanced life in the student, is a much more effective mind set to carry. That is, students need not only to matriculate their math, understand their science, or know the books of the Bible. They must be challenged to a deeper relationship with God by their studying of the Word of God. The reasonable expectation is for students to learn how to live properly with their neighbor and experience character change. Thus, it is the molding of students, not just teaching a subject, but preparing them for a life of full citizenship in the Kingdom of God that is germane.

Finally, and of specific note, just because we know a subject does not mean we are able to effectively communicate what we know. In fact, two things often do not go hand in hand. There are many gifted teachers, with highly effective communication skills who need but a few minutes to study a certain subject before they can articulate it in a very effective, concise, and enthusiastic manner. It is also true that many men and women, absolute experts in their fields of endeavor, are unable to communicate their subject at a level that students can understand. The only people they can communicate with are peers of equal or greater knowledge in the same subject.

It is important to understand and apply these principles. If teachers force feed students with too much material, they will overload them. This can easily cause discouragement and effect overall performance. Again, the goal is more than grades, or for the teacher to revel in their capability to magnificently pontificate. The goal is to ensure that our charges are able to glean from the educational experience what the teacher has learned through the teaching process. Through the unique and enthusiastic capability or gifting that God has given to the teacher, dynamic instruction for effective living is established.

Section II

The Programs

"Where there is much desire to learn, there of necessity will be much arguing, much writing, many opinions; for opinion in good men is but knowledge in the making."
John Milton, 1608-1674, The Doctrine and Discipline of Divorce (1643)

Chapter 10

The Big Picture

I have always been someone who has enjoyed an understanding of the big picture, being able to know the entire mapping of a city or how one department of an organization relates to other parts. I suppose this relates to my need to have a sense of control over my environment (some would call me a control freak). To a great extent that is a characteristic of the Western mindset, with our radical individualism. Leaders are required to ensure that all phases of a certain area of ministry are adequately managed. This could not be any truer than in the broad field of Christian Education, especially Christian education offered within a church structure.

In this section the "big picture" of Christian education will be surveyed. Brief summaries of the Christian education ministry, both inside the church and within the community at large are presented. Also provided will be some brief descriptions of the strengths and weaknesses of each area of ministry. Following, will be a more specific look at important programs for children, youth and adults. Finally, I will attempt to describe how we might integrate these various components in a positive manner within the Christian community. First, a look at the Christian school within the Christian community.

The Christian School

Because of the increased secularization of the educational system around the world and the adverse philosophical position that many public schools take, there has been an increasing need and desire for both home schooling of children as well as for the development of Private Christian schools.

As stated previously, the Word of God gives the primary responsibility for Christian education of children to the parents of those children within the Christian community. As previously discussed, in Deuteronomy 6 it states that parents are to teach their children so that they might learn the precepts of God and follow them in obedience to God's purposes.

Thus Christian education begins (hopefully) within the home. In most evangelical Christian homes, the reality is quite different. Most Christians are busy. They are focused on materialism and the negotiation of the vicissitudes of life. Thus, children are often neglected and parents are increasingly leaving the education of their children to someone outside of the home. Economic necessity and the one parent family system often prevalent in modern society necessitate assistance in the parenting process for many.

Where teaching is not possible or desirable (not many parents have the patience or capability of home schooling children) often the best alternative to an initial home education is a Christian pre-school and/or Christian primary and secondary school system. Within Christian schools, the overall philosophy of the school is clearly (or should be) Christian. However, we must be very careful to ensure that a Private Christian school is committed to an evangelical Christian worldview. Generally, the focus of these programs is to train both the mind as well as the soul and spirit of children, and to instruct them in the ways of the Lord (as well as in proper citizenship, etc.). This is accomplished along the lines of what has been already covered in this book.

Most Private Christian schools exist in conjunction with a church or a group of churches and are congregational or denominationally based. There are many virtues or blessings to Christian schools, including the unity of purpose for families, drawn together within a local community to provide for the education of their children. For many churches (The Lutherans, Anglicans and Catholics specialize in this), their education program is a missionary outreach. Often the local church must supplement the budget of the school in terms of personnel, maintenance costs etc. One of the other benefits of a Private Christian school is the usage of very expensive facilities, (i.e. the local church and their Christian education buildings) from a one to two day a week, to a six or seven day a week facility. Thus, maximum usage of the building(s) that God has provided is a demonstration of good stewardship.

The ministry of the Christian school starts with the Gospel, wanting to share Christ with children. It must also have an integrated curriculum, which includes subjects in history, science, the humanities and literature. This is also true in a home school setting where the parent is teaching his or her own children. There are many advantages to a home school. One of the advantages is the flexibility of program implementation, in that there are no pre-set hours. That is also one of the criticisms of many home school systems. Children may not learn proper discipline and socialization. It is not fully clear how true this criticism is, in that children tend to adapt to their environment with relative ease. Once they are introduced into a social setting where self-control and discipline are required, they generally adapt to societal norms in an appropriate fashion.

The central theme of the curriculum for most Christian schools is the Bible, whether presented in chapel format or catechism. Educators attempt, to the best of their ability, to integrate biblical truth into the daily life experience of the student through the organized curriculum.

Unlike secular education (which frequently attempts to mask their humanistic philosophical assumptions) they are open and blatant about their belief in the revelation of God provided to man through creation and the special revelation of God's Word. They believe that truth is absolute and that children are spiritual beings, not just physical and intellectual. Thus, the spiritual dimension of the educational program is of equal (or greater) importance.

Christian schools, as with their secular counterpart, have overall objectives they attempt to nobly fulfill. For a Christian school the key prime objective is to bring an individual student to a full knowledge of Jesus Christ and to a spiritual commitment to the Lord and his church. Further, they will have a desire to assist a child to personal maturity and growth, thus learning to take personal responsibility for their own life. Academic competence in private education is statistically above the norm of public schools. It is especially true with Christian education that the focus of education be social usefulness, academic excellence, and spiritual maturity.

In reality, the curriculum in a Private Christian school is very similar to a standard Public Education curriculum. The difference (at least for some) being the integration of biblical principles and truths into the overall curriculum.

Further, certain spiritual disciplines become a natural part of the daily activities of the school, certainly not to be found in most public schools (due to separation of church and state). These include chapel, Bible reading, prayer, praise and worship, creating an atmosphere of acceptance of our Christian lifestyle. All of these activities become an integral part of a Christian school, which helps reinforce a Christian worldview.

It should not be assumed that Christian schools are without problem. In fact, there are many criticisms leveled at Christian schools which need to be addressed. One such criticism of is that Christian schools isolate believers from the "real" world. Thus, they may have difficulty transitioning into salt and light in the community at large. This problem can be addressed very positively if it's a part of the curriculum of the school. Teachers must instruct children (or adults) not to look on those that are "in the world" as inferior human beings to Christians, thus creating a certain prejudice or religious racism. Children must simply recognize that everyone has a right and need to come to know Christ as personal Lord and Savior, and thus all have a missionary responsibility for those in the community, and to the nations of the world. Our responsibility to the world must be encouraged, and with it an integrated cross-cultural orientation, which is both beneficial and healthy. Teachers and administrators must be willing to allow students to experience the "real world", from a position of understanding and safety. Thus, the student can begin to see their place within the larger world community. Secondly, many Christian schools, due to lack of budget in many cases, feminize students. There is frequently a lack of positive male teachers, which when combined with the overemphasis on compliance and lack of individual differentiation (seen in the overemphasis on correct behavior, never fight, never criticize, be nice at all times; unrealistic expectations) tend to produce boys and girls unprepared for life in the public arena. How tragic to see children go from Christian pre-school (or home school) to Christian School, to Christian College to the real world, only to see them lost to the church due to an inability to interface with and manage the temptations of a secular society.

Finally, again due to the inherent budget restraints most Christian schools labor under, the materials and curriculum necessary for students to compete are lacking. Computer labs, Science labs, etc. are needed and hard to supply in a small though highly dedicated school. Community partnerships must be developed if the legitimate needs of a student body are to be reasonably met.

Organization of A Christian School

When organizing a Christian school, whether pre-school, a regular K-12 program, a Bible college or institute, or a support program for home-schoolers, the key person in that process is always the Pastor(s).[9] The pastor must have, as a part of his or her vision, a desire for the education of all people form birth to grave. The church school, under the pastor's vision, most likely will have a Minister of Education or a board of education who will give care to the concerns of the parents and students, providing governance and oversight to the educational ministry. If established as a Board of Education, the pastor or Minister of Education will have people from the local church and perhaps from the outside community who offer counsel and expertise in areas needed for the local school.

In most states a school must be registered though the Department of Education in the local county, which usually is a fairly easy task.

---

[9] In many communities, several pastors and churches may come together to create a community school. This is a healthy trend, breeding unity and cooperative effort. Still, some one has to have a vision for the program, and take the lead.

Then a curriculum must be chosen, teachers found, classrooms assigned, etc. This is a tremendous task, rife with pitfalls and problems to be overcome. Fortunately, there are outstanding educational ministries that are readily available who will assist in the development of a Christian school within a local church community.

As our society continues to become more secularized, the need for Christian schools will likely grow. This growth must not be for the sake of being different alone, but to address legitimate need for an alternative to deteriorating public school programs.

About Teaching Adults

Along with educational services for children, there is a growing trend and perceived need for the education of adults. Adult education includes both the highly practical as well as the biblical and theological.

Briefly, Adult Christian Education should be comprised of two fundamental and foundational components. They are the practical education and training of families in daily living, from birth to grave, and theological or biblical education.

A family ministry curriculum will provide courses in adult education that are practical and relevant to the needs of the community. Such courses as Marriage and Family Life, Communication Skills, Single Parenting, Financial Planning and Divorce and Remarriage are needed. These courses can be offered, usually at very little cost, and are often provided by Christian experts within the local community. These training courses can significantly enhance the overall growth and development of the adults within a caring Christian community, as well as provide evangelistic opportunities for the community at large.

Christian parenting is one of the biggest needs in society, especially in light of society's numerous ills. The increase in domestic violence and child abuse is abhorrent, even in Christian circles, and can be eradicated to a great extent by education and support systems that the church of the locality[10] can provide. Unfortunately, the church has, by and large, neglected confronting these issues from a biblical perspective. There is a crying need to have practical curriculum as a part of the adult education program to address the growing needs of a secularized culture. Further, a part of a practical curriculum will include the standard adult Sunday school level courses in biblical studies, such as the study of a certain book of the Bible or various topics and themes within the Word of God that every believer needs to understand. This can include foundational courses such as a new believer's class, courses in Old Testament and New Testament, as well as courses discussing issues of importance such as the Fruit of the Spirit, the Gifts of the Holy Spirit, etc.

Along with practical studies, and in light of the churches responsibility to train present and future leaders, there is a need for a Bible Institute or College. Adults are hungry to be trained in Biblical studies and Theology. Unfortunately, the standard models of seminary training are out of the reach of the average Christian. George Barna, President of The Barna Institute reports (as presented in the provisional catalog of the new Wagner Leadership Institute, 1998) that "most pastors agree that they were inadequately trained for the job of leading the local church. Yet, seminaries continue to forge ahead, providing much of the same irrelevant (and in some cases, misleading and harmful) education that has been their forte for the past century. One response has been churches creating their own ministry education centers to raise up leaders and teachers from within their congregations. Another response has been for churches to hire believers who have secular training and experience in a professional field and allow them to learn the content of ministry realities while they are on the job. There is little doubt that churches are in desperate need of effective leadership as the challenges

---

[10] When I refer to the church of the locality, I am specifically addressing the possible unified consortium that can and should be developed in local communities, where churches of all types band together for a greater purpose, whether for missions, education or evangelistic outreach.

confronting the Church become more complex, more numerous and more daunting.

But how will those leaders be identified, developed and nurtured for effective ministry leadership? Is there a role for the seminary in the future of the church? If so, what should that seminary look like and what would its ideal role be? If churches continue to rely on seminaries--or some alternative developmental structure--to provide them with leaders, it is imperative that the leader training grounds be reshaped. Mere tinkering with a broken system won't provide the answer; creating a holistic, strategic and intelligently-crafted process is needed." This indictment, against the White Elephant of standard seminary education has resulted in many new and exciting adaptations.

Adult education can be extremely effective and provided at low cost. Many new paradigm institutions within the United States have developed such alternative services. From video based programs to complete Bible College and Theological training courses, advanced education for ministry and leadership can be made available to a local church as a part of an extension from an existing College or Institute. These systems can be implemented in a cost-effective way, becoming a tremendous blessing for the local community. Multi-cultural programs are readily available in numerous formats. Generally, local faculty can train leadership for a church or a group of churches, developing men and women in their areas of gifting, many of which may become church workers, church planters, or members of church staffs as full-time ministers.

God has given a mandate to leaders in the Body of Christ to train and educate God's precious people from birth to grave, (Eph. 4:11-17). The learning process never ends. All education and training programs are designed to prepare God's people for future life with him, when believers will rule and reign with Christ. Thus, educational efforts, to include training within the church of the locality must be seen through the eyes of eternal results, from an eschatological and Kingdom perspective.

The Developmental Stages

Much has been written on the topic of human development. Any student who is interested in a greater understanding of human growth and development should read Dr. Joseph Bohac's book *"Human Development: A Christian Perspective."* It is important information that can be used for the proper grouping of students based upon their developmental needs.

Applied human development is a component of public and private schools, Christian and non-Christian, as well as Sunday school programs. What is presented here is to assist in the grouping of students for effective education.

Nursery School Age Group

The first grouping of students would be that of the nursery school. This typically consists of children three years of age and under. The focus of teaching nursery school is to provide loving care of these children and the development of pre-learning skills though simple play, singing songs and doing age appropriate projects. The younger the child, the less they are able to participate in the learning activities. The closer a child comes to age three, the more they become able to develop pre-learning capabilities. Thus they can learn simple songs, and will greatly benefit from stories read to them, while developing and practicing their large motor skills through play.

The Beginner

The beginner's age, which corresponds with ages three to five, is a stage of primary concrete mental operations.

The physical characteristics of this age group are that of rapid physical and intellectual growth. It is a restless age. That is, children age three to five are in almost constant motion, with lives filled with play and continuous curiosity with all that pertains to them. Any teacher that has tried to change or control a child at this age has usually experienced tremendous frustration. In fact, the primary methodology of teaching for this age is to continuously change the instruction or the environment in order to redirect the abundant energies of the child. Key goals include teaching basic cooperation, while recognizing that children have less than a six-minute attention span. Teaching is done in small bites, as comprehension is low, enhanced by multiple repetition.

In terms of their mental and emotional qualities, children this age can only give attention in spurts. They have a distinct impulse to play. So it is best to use that natural innate impulse for the glory of God. Make games with hands, feet, etc. and direct their minds along positive lines through correcting behavior as it comes. Often they will learn by observation; they have vivid imaginations. Thus, a teacher will want to capitalize on this gift. They can use hankies for doll beds, sails for boats, etc. Vocabulary is quite limited so be careful not to use big words. Most three-year-olds have a vocabulary of approximately 900 picture words. Children this age tend towards a degree of stranger anxiety. Making the classroom as comfortable as possible while ensuring safety is essential.

The spiritual capacities of this age vary. Many will have questions about God and heaven. They have a tremendous capacity for simple faith, much more so than adults do. They forget differences quickly and do not hold grudges, which makes it a wonderful age to work with. Their spiritual lives can be easily molded because they believe that they are cared for and will quickly forgive, even when we make mistakes towards them.

Some of the special interests and problems of this age group include an acute interest in nature. For them, the world is a grand wonderland. Thus, they love stories about nature (God's creation), the childhoods of different cultures (including biblical stories) and especially tales on various aspects of the life of Jesus. A teacher will attempt to make stories to fit their age. Teaching them how to function in their home, how to respect parents, how to share etc. are illustrative of the curriculums of this group. They learn how to express themselves within the classroom and tend to be quite expressive. They will say the first thing that comes to mind so don't be surprised if, when asked how are things at home, they reveal the details of mom and dad's argument from that morning.

In terms of the class, it's important to allow these children to play using object lessons, singing, stories of life, etc. and have activities that frequently change over short periods of time. All children love attention (which is one of the reasons for temper tantrums). Teachers must recognize that they play a very vital in the life of the child. So whether in a primary school, that of a Sunday school program, or even in a specialized one-week curriculum of a vacation Bible school, it's most important to keep the above points in mind.

Primary Age Group

The next stage is that of the primary student, ages 6-8 inclusive. This stage is often referred to as the affectionate age. Physically, boys and girls are very similar in need to those of the beginner age, but with larger sizes and more developed fine and gross motor coordination. Their mental and emotional qualities include both learning and reading. This enables them to begin learning how to reason. Their thinking is still quite concrete (black and white, right or wrong, good or evil). Their understanding of rules and justice is overt with very limited abstract reasoning capability.

In fact, their thinking is quite black and white as illustrated by the phrase that "good things happen to good people and bad things happen to bad people." So they tend to personalize or interject bad things that happen in their world on to themselves. That is, when something pertaining to them goes wrong, they believe something must be innately wrong with them. Thus one of the dangers in telling stories, at this age or younger, about demonic activity is that they cannot understand nor handle the concept, especially in light of their vivid imagination.

During this age, children have a beginning ability to differentiate between fact and fantasy, to begin to recognize truth. They have a tremendous curiosity and a pronounced need for affection, both the desire to give and to receive. They have tremendous imaginative powers. Children of this age tend to respond well to good habits such as cleanliness, church attendance, eating, sleeping, etc.

Six year olds have a vocabulary of approximately twenty-five hundred words, which is increasing at a very rapid rate. Spiritually they have many questions about God. They have a wonderful capacity for faith as at an earlier age, they do not hold grudges, are able to forgive quickly. They continue with the desire to experience life, and are desperately desirous to please significant others. In light of this, they tend towards hero worship, choosing role models after their own self-image. Teachers naturally become the heroes for the students. In fact, many of the students will "fall in love" with their teacher. This is nothing to be terribly frightened about, they pass through it fairly well. It just shows the intensity of their emotional involvement with their learning environment.

Just as with the beginner age, primary's respond well to real life stories. They are beginning to understand how things work and what goes on behind closed doors. It's very important to be open to their questions, willing to respond to them in a direct, non-plussed fashion. At the same time, do not try and "protect" a child by not telling them the whole truth. As they grow up, they will learn to resent distortion (such as Santa Claus, etc.).

Junior

The next age group is the junior age, ages nine through eleven. The physical characteristics of the junior are slower growth yet increased vigor and energy. It is a time of rapid brain development. Though they are conserving their strength for adolescence, they are made to blow off steam.

Emerging mental and emotional qualities include that fact, not fantasy, are most important. They have a strong, inquisitive nature, now met through more advanced and complex reading skills. They will enjoy reading if they have learned basic reading skills. Also, competition for attention, social status and academic achievement becomes intense. Junior girls' still climb trees and boys will try to out climb them. There is very little difference between the sexes. They have a strong sense of fair play and justice. Therefore, their parents must be wise and fair. It's an age of advanced memory development, combined with a loss of imaginative powers, as they become increasingly independent.

Spiritually, Juniors have a heart that is truly open to the Lord. They will begin to see and experience the consequences of conduct, both good and bad. Their own conduct which does not align with internalized standards of right and wrong will weigh heavily upon them, exhibited as guilt or shame. The highest percentage of souls being won to Christ occurs during this age. This is due to the emerging ability to see how life can be ruined by sin. Key and critical habits are being formed at this age, thus the importance of teaching good and healthy habits. Finally, respect for authority, the need to be friendly and kind to others, the importance of taking care of the downtrodden, are all essential components of their emerging sensibilities. Much of the impressions and perceptions formed during this age will be remembered and acted on throughout the rest of their life.

This is one of the reasons they can relate to the real life stories (especially of heroes) of Jesus, David, Samuel, Esther, etc. Autobiographies are delightful for them to read, as they develop a sense of history. Thus, it's important to teach Bible history. Customs, habits, and manners of biblical life are of high interest to students at this age. They have a hunger and thirst for real knowledge. Bible studies and "sword drills" can be a great benefit and fun for this age group.

Intermediary

The next stage is that of the 12 through 14-year-old adolescent called the intermediary age. This age is also known as the gateway age. The physical characteristics of this latency age and early adolescent period has characteristics of growth including rapid and uneven growth, with a high degree of laziness and social and physical awkwardness. Puberty and sexual arousal begin sometime during these years, beginning the change from childhood to adulthood. It is an age of great change and self-consciousness. Girls are usually about a year ahead of boys in terms of their overall development.

In terms of their mental activity, self-feeling is highly aroused. They begin to develop a sense of ego or self with characteristic natural vanity. They have an overly sensitive desire to look their very best. They have a highly developed sense of humor with and can enjoy a good joke, as long as they are not the subject of the joke. It's difficult to get them to take things seriously. Often, a teacher will find them to be stubborn and quite "squirrelly." This is a very difficult phase for most parents to deal with, though it can be a fascinating time of growth and change. They are full of life, love thrills and still carry a form of hero worship for parents and teachers. Often a teacher will see a high variability in overall intellectual capability, which begins to manifest during this stage. Thus, a teacher must stay on their toes, remaining flexible in terms of the teaching process.

There are many varied interests and problems that this age group must face. The most important of which is that crucial ideals are being formulated. Providing high ideals and frank information about issues of life is critical. Since habits are being formed, hopefully positive, the need to teach them how to pray, prepare for major life decisions (such as marriage, vocational decisions, etc.) and relationship development in general is imperative. This is also a time where very negative habits can begin, such as swearing, smoking, drinking and drugs. Therefore, leading the young person to Christ is a prime concern and objective. If the child is a Christian, the focus should be on continuing and solidifying their commitment to the Lord.

Again, using examples from real life are helpful. Using real biblical illustrations such as Daniel and Joseph, who demonstrate a life of purity and fidelity, with the ability, in spite of weaknesses, to overcome adversity are to be emphasized. It is still best to have separate classes for instruction because of the high sexual energy and tension within male and female relationships. They often will mutually repel each other, which in some ways is quite good, but can also create a dynamic within a classroom that can be most difficult.

In terms of activities, they usually prefer local clubs, physical activities and enjoy sports. They still need significant help and advice, both from parents and teachers, even if they do not actively seek it. If teachers are able to develop a positive relationship with them, their influence can be used of God to help if troubles arise.

Senior High

The next stage is Seniors, which corresponds to ages 15-17+ exclusive, the age of *life choices*. Physically, Seniors will likely obtain full height and weight. Their brain growth is complete and their physical stature has become primarily fixed. The full attainment of puberty is usually reached by age 17.

The later adolescents' mental and emotional qualities include a reaction against the general mores of the previous generation. This will be seen in their unique (some times boarding on the bizarre, though thankfully mostly transitory) habits and expressions. Making critical life choices based on clear information and individual gifting is attempted. This includes, for most, choices regarding future vocation, mates, education, etc.

During this rather arbitrary and market driven age (prior to the turn of the 20th century, most adolescents were classified as adults, with adult expectations and responsibilities) emotions can run quite high, with dramatic, nearly daily shifts in mood. Sexual and other tensions and temptations can be strong, as will their sense of ethics and fair play. Their ability to think and reason makes them acute observers of their surroundings. Therefore, they can be quite critical of the inconsistencies of adults. They tend towards faultfinding with adult beliefs (especially dogmatic expressions of the same) and behaviors, without the ability to comprehend intent. It's quite a romantic age, a time of daydreaming, chivalry, and of conquering, with idyllic dreams of greatness for the future. Men want to rescue women, and often women want to be rescued by men.

There is also an emerging spiritual hunger that manifests in the older adolescent, much greater than most people realize. Most young people raised in the church are well aware of biblical principles and how to apply them to life. However, teachers need to continue to guide and encourage them in their relationship with Christ. Hopefully, altruistic motivations will emerge, focusing on increased fidelity and a sense of responsibility to care for others. Generally, faith can be quite strong, and their desire to serve God can be incredibly intense and zealous. This zealousness should be encouraged but not exploited.

Special interests and problems in this age revolve around relationships. Friendship in relationships should be emphasized, not exclusivity. Parents need to give advice as to what their Seniors watch on TV and read (mainly, encourage much more reading and less TV watching), as well as to the social environment that they are involved in. Advice does not mean control, as the teacher and the parent alike must take on the role of coach, not dictator. Scripture states that children are to obey their parents; young people are to learn as with all adults to honor their parents. Honoring emerges from parental sharing and caring, not by demanding blind obedience (the later does not work anyway). Realize that young people are looking for a legitimate challenge to live a truly committed life for Christ.

Ultimately, in terms of class activities, teaching Bible lessons and the doctrines of Christ are needed. Class size should be kept to a maximum of twenty students where possible. The teacher must be sympathetic and understanding in order to help the students build a foundation for their future. He or she must be kind, firm and ready to deal with problems that will inevitably arise, especially in the area of sexual or spiritual concerns.

Young Adults

The educational process continues, or at least should, throughout the rest of life. The next stage of development is that of young adults, ages 18-24. This time of life is called the ***mountain top*** age. Physical maturity has been reached for most, and the major decisions of marriage, vocational choices, etc. are being negotiated. The young adult is becoming much more mature and rounded in personality, though still struggles with important life issues as noted above.

Young adults have an ability to tease and rebel against strong dogmatic or highly religious rules and regulations. Because of their intellectual capabilities and deep desire for intimacy along with closeness and meaning in relationships, most of the curriculum developed for this age group must focus on relational wholeness. The young man or woman's relationship to church, God, the opposite sex, work, etc., should be addressed with frankness and openness. Further, vocational choices, being so very critical to success in life, are often topics for instruction and dialog.

Further, strong convictions are being formed, hopefully in a positive vein towards Christ and the church. Thus, it can be one of the periods of greatest service for Christ. Sincere life commitments in this age group can lead to full-time Christian ministry. Even if full-time ministry is not the goal for a specific young adult, encouragement to serve the Lord in a lay capacity should be emphasized. If service for of the Lord does not begin at this age, it seldom will in later life. To live is to serve, and young adults, with their abundance of energy and enthusiasm have an ability to give and receive help for spiritual life problems. Thus, a strong emphasis on teaching the Bible with practical life application is of greatest benefit.

This brief description of development lays a foundation for understanding the needs and special concerns of the various age groups. As educators we must recognize that each developmental stage has differing needs that must be addressed in creating an effective educational ministry for the local church.

"Whoso neglects learning in his youth loses the past and is dead for the future."
Euripides, Phrixus,
Fragment 927

Chapter 11

Children

When thinking of children's programs, there are three primary venues that come to mind. First is the Sunday school. Secondly, children's church. And thirdly, specialized evangelism programs such as Vacation Bible Schools. There are many programs that have been designed for children including entertainment programs, puppetry, video-based instruction, etc, but are beyond the scope of this book.

Most leaders recognize the mandate from the Lord to teach and train children. To say it better, it is to train and to teach children. Training must always precede teaching. Discipline is necessary for learning to occur. Every teacher will echo that reality. In understanding the ministry of education to children, we will first look at Sunday schools and their place in the present scheme of life in the local church.

Sunday School

The modern Sunday school as we know it was born in Gloucester, England in the eighteenth century. Robert Raikes, who is generally credited with founding the Sunday school movement, worked thirty years to reform criminals. After many years of hard and frustrating work, he concluded that an ounce of prevention was better than a pound of cure. How true. Unfortunately, few friends or religious leaders of his day were found to give support or encouragement to his belief. His friends dubbed him and his Sunday school, "Bobby," "wild-goose" and his "ragged regiment." However, within four years of his beginning, Sunday schools in the United Kingdom had a membership of nearly 250,000 children.

Mr. Raikes soon found a powerful ally in the great reformer John Wesley. Wesley recognized the positive impact of the Sunday school and immediately incorporated it into his program of ministry. The Methodist church and the evangelical church at large owes a debt of gratitude to Mr. Raikes, for his Sunday school programs were foundational to the early success of this great movement. Wesley wrote, "I think these Sunday schools are the noble institutions which have been needed in Europe for some centuries and will increase more and more provided the teachers and instructors do their duties." The Sunday school movement spread rapidly in the United Kingdom and eventually came to America where it has achieved its greatest growth.

In 1791 the first Sunday school society was formed in Philadelphia, Pennsylvania. This was the beginning of a most influential program for church growth in America. In fact, much of the success of the churches growth in the United States can be traced to the Sunday school. No group has been more successful in the development and the usage of Sunday school programs for the evangelization of America as has the Baptist denominational groups. From their bus ministries to their special Sunday school programs, they have lead the way in the development of highly effective Sunday school outreaches. Many of these programs continue today and have been adapted by many other denominational and non-denominational groups alike.

The modern Sunday school was not the first such attempt to educate children in the Word of God. From the days of Ezra (approximately) it was the custom of the Jews to assemble in their place of teaching, often called the Synagogue, for instruction. This was done to hear the law and learn to make practical application of its meaning. The teaching of the Word of God was primarily for male students, though girls were often taught at home under the tutelage of their mothers. The Jews have continued to see the importance of this training and require no less than 325 hours of instruction a year. The Roman Catholic Church, who to a great extent has adopted the Yeshiva style of instruction, requires 200 hours a year of Catechism or training. They consider it a vital part of the maintenance of their movements.

It's estimated that untrained teachers and irregular attendance has reduced the Protestant attendance of Sunday school to an average of 17 hours a year. As much as two thirds of children spend no time in a Sunday school program.

The Sunday school has been the greatest universal means in modern times of reaching children for God. It is during the early childhood ages, as has been previously discussed that children are most vulnerable to the truths of the Gospel of Jesus Christ. Often, Sunday is a day for children to play, but they are also looking for structure, love and nurturing, which can be readily provided within the Sunday school environment. Biblically, the Sunday school exists because of what the Word of God states in Deuteronomy 31:12-13,

> *"Gather the people together, men and women and children and the stranger that is within your gates that they may hear and that they may learn and fear the Lord your God and observe to do all the works of the law. And that their children which have not known anything, may hear and learn to fear the Lord your God as you live in the land where you are going over Jordan to possess it."*

> Matthew 28:19-20 says, *"Go therefore and make disciples of all the nations, baptizing them in the name of the Father and the Son and the Holy Spirit, teaching them to observe all that I commanded you; and lo, I am with you always, even to the end of the age."*

In other words, the focus of teaching and training within the home and church is to equip God's people so that they can fear God and follow his Word all the days of their lives. Whether this process of education is done in the form of a Sunday school curriculum is a local community's option. If chosen, it must focus on its historical goals.

Thus, the ministry of the Sunday school is first of all evangelistic. To reach young people with the gospel of Jesus Christ is its primary goal. Secondarily, the Sunday school can be used to supplement the training of children in the ways of God in support of the parents' responsibility. The hope is that the principles taught in Sunday school will lay a strong foundation of faith that will sustain them as they grow to maturity.

It is apparent to most that there is a need for Sunday school programs, or at least some sort of Christian education for children. There are many modifications of the Sunday school, including Saturday schools and backyard evangelism ministry. Ultimately, the church must be involved in the education of children. The key to an effective children's ministry, and one of the greatest difficulties of the Sunday school movement is finding dedicated Christian leaders who will be able to effectively minister with dedication and consistency to children.

For the sake of understanding, it is important to review the organizational structure of the Sunday school. As with any successful program in a local church, the most important person is the pastor of the church. Sunday school is not the pastor's school. Though he or she is ultimately responsible for it, they can nor will be the primary leaders of the Sunday school. However, ministry to children must be a part of the pastor's vision. When a pastor sees the children as a bother or simply a difficult task that must be managed, that attitude will be felt by the workers and ultimately the parents and children. A pastor must have an enthusiastic desire for the Sunday school program and be willing to promote that program enthusiastically.

Secondly, the pastor needs to be watchful of the Sunday school ministry, giving it proper priority within the overall structure of the church. As such, the pastor should involve him or herself with the teaching and training or ensuring that the task is being done effectively and efficiently. Showing interest in the classes, the students and the teachers is very important. As a pastor in charge of Christian education ministry, it was partially my task, on behalf of the senior pastor, to ensure that the Sunday school program ran smoothly. However, when I became a Senior Pastor, it was perceived and received as a great blessing and a strong statement of support when I would come to a classroom and observe, showing my interest in the teacher and the children. Along with personal support and enthusiastic promotion, a pastor must be able to work well with the chosen leaders and the teaching staff, while ensuring that there is proper equipment and facilities available to minister effectively to the children.

The pastor should also be actively involved in the evaluation of proper curriculum for their students. As a Christian educator, we strongly recommend the curriculum developed by Bishop Dr. Paul Paino and Calvary Ministries International, Fort Wayne, Indiana. (For more on their curriculum, see the appendix.) This dynamic ministry has developed a comprehensive educational system that can be used over and over again, saving literally thousands of dollars in the purchase of curriculum materials for students. It's an excellent program, one of many excellent programs available. The **_School for the Bible_** Sunday school curriculum is highly recommended as a cost effective and comprehensive system for any local church.

Assisting and supporting the pastor, if it is a large church, is a Director of Christian Education or a pastor in charge of Christian Education. This leader gives the overall direction to all areas of education within the ministry of the church. However, the key person in the actual development of the Children's Church program is what is commonly known as the Sunday School Superintendent.

The Super

The essential qualities of a good Sunday school superintendent include some of the following. First, they should be a sincere, preferably positive and happy Christian. I have seen many Sunday school superintendents who were sour in disposition, having built their own little kingdom within the local church. They may have been enthusiastic at one time, but have lost their joy along the line. There is no room for sour and dower leadership in this vital position.

The Sunday school superintendent must have the respect of the pastor and the Sunday school staff, as well as the parents of the children they minister to. As with all areas of service in the Body of Christ, it is essential that they be a team player, possessing enthusiasm and able to promote good relationships within their department. As a leader they must give and receive input, feedback and suggestions in a willing way. They are to give the work of Sunday school their highest priority in terms of their ministry within the local church.

As with any leader they must set a biblical example in lifestyle, showing love and appreciation for the people of God, especially the teachers and students they will be working with. Thus, they must learn to be tactful, because they will be working with a wide variety of different personalities, often needing tender loving care to keep them on task. Obviously, they should be faithful in their own attendance in church, recognizing that they are first of all Christians and secondly workers.

The ability to work well with the pastor under the church structure while formulating and promoting a solid Sunday school program is the goal. This is not always easy in light of the numerous choices to be made in terms of curriculum and types of services. It seems that, as in psychology, everybody has an opinion about something. This is especially true with Sunday schools (and Little League!). Thus, the superintendent or Children's Church director must be a fairly strong personality and yet flexible enough to listen and care about the opinions of others.

As the overseer of the Children's educational program, the facilities and materials for instruction are of great concern. The Super must ensure that the buildings and internal facilities of the Sunday school or Children's church are open, clean and available at the time the program is to begin. There is nothing more discouraging to a teacher than to have to hunt down supplies or rearrange a classroom prior to beginning a class session. The Super is to oversee the facilitation of the educational program in cooperation with the maintenance department, etc.

Along with insuring that facilities and materials are available, the Super is responsible to oversee the Sunday school or Children's church schedule while in session. A "hands on" method of supervision is generally best. As a Sunday school superintendent or Children's church director, it's difficult to supervise while teaching a class, all-though it can be done if one has a good assistant to work with. What seems to be best is for the superintendent or Children's church director to function as a floating principal, giving guidance and support to the teachers, assisting when problems arise, willing to step in to give extra support when required.

It is helpful to touch as many of the children as you can. Touching them on the head and/or shoulder lets the children know that they are loved and that the teachers are there for them. Also, giving kind words of encouragement to the teachers is wise. Visiting every classroom every Sunday is most positive and helpful, which is for a greater purpose than merely taking attendance. A Superintendents presence will show support and care for the teachers and their labor for good within the classroom.

A continual responsibility under the Superintendents supervision is the follow-up work, tracking and including new children that attend the Sunday school. Each Sunday new children are likely to come to the Sunday school or Children's church program. A positive and effective follow-up program can win many of these children to Christ, and if the children are reached, so can their parents. Many families have been reached for Christ through the initial door of the Sunday school. A good follow-up system, including thank you cards and a phone call to the child and their parents can be effective.

Another responsibility of the Super, one of the more difficult aspects of this all-volunteer ministry is the need to continuously recruit and train teachers. This need must be kept at the forefront of the church. Recruiting is a continuous task, and the Super must always be on the look out for potential teachers. Further, regular and professional training of the teachers will keep the them fresh and motivated. Rewarding the teachers with regular thanks and recognition awards will keep them involved in this vital ministry. Thus, Supers should be actively involved in a continuous process of recruiting new teachers and training them so that they are available for the educational needs of the children.

Personal Requirements

Prior to taking on the responsibility of a Sunday school director, the leader should know how to organize a Sunday school or Children's church program. Where organizational skills are lacking, there are conferences available or other churches within the local community that already have highly effective Sunday school and Children's church programs where these skills can be obtained. It is perfectly legitimate to seek support and assistance from outside sources and to evaluate other programs, adapting them to ones' local church setting. Trying to recreate the wheel is difficult and mostly unnecessary.

Also, the Director must understand what the qualifications of teachers and secretaries are to ensure that the right people are placed in key positions. A basic understanding of teaching methods, aims, and principles is needed. Some of these have been discussed earlier in this book. Further, a Director must have a sense that their ministry is of vital importance. Each individual in educational ministry are special emissaries of Christ himself, representing the local church and pastor, ministering to the precious children under their charge. Thus, from the opening of a Sunday service, where they assist in leading worship, through the supervision of the program, the Superintendent is a key leader in the church. Ultimately, the leader of this department acts as an associate minister, sharing one of the largest burdens of a local church. The responsibility is awesome as this ministry effects positively so many in the church. The Super is of high value for the church and the Kingdom of God.

Because of the many varied tasks and responsibilities presented above, every superintendent must keep fresh their personal relationship with the Lord. The greater our intimacy with the Lord the more effective our ministry. The Super, as with every other minister in the church, must seek God's guidance in every aspect of life. The Word of God is to remain a precious part of our daily life, as prayer and the study of the Word is our very lifeline. It is so easy to become bogged down with the busyness of living a Christian life, whether a parent, as a worker, let alone as a volunteer director of a Children's church or Sunday school program. Keeping our priorities clear, which includes the daily study of God's Word is a key to our sanity and growth.

The Sunday School Secretary

It has been aptly stated that the job is not over until the paperwork is done. In most Sunday school/Children's church programs there must be someone available to handle the multiplied paperwork generated. A well organized, somewhat compulsive secretary can cover a multitude of needs. There are many tasks to be accomplished by the Sunday school secretary. Before reviewing the tasks of a secretary, an ideal picture of a secretary is needed. First of all, a good Sunday school secretary will have a pleasant, even temperament, and a love for children. Secondly, they will have an ability to keep track of the records of the Sunday school/Children's church program, which includes attendance, offerings, salvations, baptisms, and every other aspect of the Sunday school/Children's church program.

A good secretary is one who can work alongside the superintendent, anticipating the needs of the Sunday school program for him/her as well as for the teachers. In most cases, they are actively involved in the ordering of textbook and other classroom materials for the Sunday school/Children's church programs. (This is unnecessary for her if the *"School of the Bible,"* is available in the local Church; see appendix).

The secretary must be familiar with the various types of literature that are needed for each grade level. It is acknowledged as a true gift to the pastor as well to the local assembly when neat and accurate records of the Sunday school/Children's church ministry are created and maintained.

As a part of the staff, the secretary should attend all conference and training classes. He or she should be willing to be trained in higher administrative functions. In many cases, this person becomes the "heir-apparent" of the Sunday school/Children's church department. A good secretary is worth their weight in gold and should be well taken care of both personally and spiritually.

The Sunday School Teacher

While much has already been said regarding teachers, the importance of teaching methods and personal character issues, it is helpful to review these in light of the special requirements of a Sunday school program.

A good Sunday school teacher should be a Christian with a positive personal testimony of their life in Christ. They should have a love for children, their parents and for teaching, and possess enough patience to peacefully teach rambunctious children. The Bible does say that the trials of our faith works patience and believe me, if you are working in the Sunday school/Children's church program you will have the opportunity to experience many trials, which will ultimately lead to patience (or insanity!).

A good teacher must have a hunger for and growing knowledge of the Word of God, able to apply God's Word in practical situations. The teacher needs to be enthusiastic and faithful in their attendance and work for the Lord. When children come to class, they are extremely enthusiastic and excited about being there.

Teachers in Sunday school need to be aware that many children bring problems with them from home. It's not unusual to hear very unique and interesting conversations between children about what happened Saturday night, or even Sunday morning on their way to church. Having good "listening" ears with grace and discernment (you cannot always believe what children say as they have the gift of exaggeration) can help you minister more poignantly to children.

The ultimate goal is to win each young person to Christ and to disciple them into Christ-likeness. That is, the goal is to fulfill the Great Commission as presented in Matthew 28.

Top 10 List

Provided here is a list of 10 good rules for a successful Sunday school/Children's church instructor that can help the superintendent to know the kind of person to look for as well as how to effectively evaluate a good versus inadequate Sunday school/Children's church worker. This is only a guide, as perfect candidates will rarely if ever be found.

The first and foremost rule of teaching is **being prepared**. You can generally tell the difference when someone has waited until late Saturday night or early Sunday morning to prepare their lesson. A conscientious teacher will take the necessary time to prepare both spiritually as well as logistically for the class to be presented.

Secondly, the teachers will allow God to **prepare their heart** for the task. This includes spending as much time as possible in prayer and preparation, especially praying for the students that are in their charge.

Number three, a good teacher will attempt to make each **lesson** as **interesting and relevant** as possible. A teacher should add lots of spice and illustrations to their lessons wherever possible. Children are always fascinated by personal illustrations, so as much as possible, and as long as it is appropriate to the lesson and not too revealing, personal illustrations are most helpful.

Fourth, teachers are to **attract the attention** of young scholars. Presenting the lesson in a positive and enthusiastic manner with the anointing of the Holy Spirit is the key. Using illustrations can be helpful. If the topic is communion, actually having communion in the class with the children demonstrates its importance.

Number five is **be personal** with the class. A teacher must be able to communicate at the same level of comprehension as the students.

An instructor must be firm, but also friendly. Warmth goes a long way in the teaching environment.

Number six is to **stay in touch** with each individual student. It's helpful, if possible, to visit a child's home. This is sometimes difficult in light of logistics within a city, but if a visit is possible one can get a greater feel for the life experience of each child and be able to minister to them more effectively.

Number seven is to **never be late or absent** if at all possible. Situations can occur which make it impossible to be at your class. But wherever possible, be there early to greet the children with a smile and a hug, which helps start the day.

Number eight is to **leave your personal life at home**. The classroom is never a place to share the difficulties of our life with the students. This is not to state that if one has a cold to not ask the students to pray for healing. That is a very positive way to involve them in learning to minister to others. But if a teacher has had a fight with their spouse, or is having conflict with the local church pastor, by all means avoid bringing that into the classroom.

Number nine is to have some **goals** in mind for the class. The goals include such things as salvation, the infilling of the Holy Spirit, etc. for each child. The goals may include memorizing a certain percentage of verses during a quarter. Also, the teachers' goal is to prepare their children for next years' class, so that when the next teacher inherits the children they will be able to say categorically that these children have been well prepared by the previous teacher.

Number 10 is to always remember that **children are** always **watching** us. Teachers are always discipling someone. The children are most perceptive. We cannot just turn on being a wonderful loving Christian teacher then turn it off after walking out of the class. Often students will see their teacher in the real world and do a quick comparison between the teacher, their parents and other adults they are in relationship with. They need to see a consistent Christian pattern. All believers and everyone in leadership should be equally concerned about a consistent testimony, but it's especially true with Sunday school/Children's church workers.

Practical Wisdom

To summarize and conclude this section on ministry to children, there are several brief points of wisdom to be shared. Remember that all children are not alike. Children are constantly changing. Their moods change, their thoughts and beliefs can change and we are to be part of their positive change as we teach the curriculum and exhibit a godly lifestyle.

Also, children are not just young adults. Therefore, we must be able to talk to a child at a level that they are able to understand. Many adults will either speak down to children in a childish manner, which is inappropriate, or speak over their head using words that the child cannot understand (especially bible words like sanctification, justification, propitiation, etc.). Thus, we have to know our audience and speak to them clearly and concisely, according to their level of comprehension.

Further, it should be acknowledged that children, especially other parents' children, are strange creatures. They can be silly, hyperactive, squirrelly, unappreciative, aggressive, coy, shy, etc., but they are none of those things. They are individuals created in the image of God and thus must be treated as individuals with love and respect.

For children, it is fun to learn. It is natural for children to explore and understand new things. If a teacher makes the class a boring prison, devoid of stimulation other than the pontification of the teacher, it becomes virtually unbearable. Make it exciting with lots of changes, new programs and a lot of fun. Children not only like to learn, but they will learn very rapidly unless we as the teacher drive the desire to learn from them.

Children also have many questions. No question is a bad question. Questions like, "Who made God?" are not unusual. Also, questions about the uncertainty of life are frequent with children. Teachers must be willing to listen carefully and answer questions with simplicity and wisdom. If we do not know the answer, it is perfectly acceptable to tell a child, "I'm not sure about that yet, but I will get back to you later." And if the promise is made, make sure it is kept!

Children are constantly moving from a state of dependence to independence. The ultimate goal is for them to become independent enough to choose interdependence or covenant relationships once adulthood is achieved. A large part of the Children's church ministry and later youth ministry, is designed not just to keep the children from harm or protect them from the world, but to proactively provide for them information, inspiration and understanding of how to live the Christian life with courage and divine purpose. Sunday school is a time honored and vital ministry of the church that can lay a foundation for a life of loving and fruitful service for the Lord.

"Ask the young; they know everything!"
Joseph Joubert, 1754-1824

Chapter 12

Youth

When discussing youth ministry, the most important thing to remember is that young people (teenagers) are stuck between childhood and adulthood. They are in a most precarious time of life. Major decisions effecting their future are being made. Bodily changes are occurring at a break neck pace. There is a great need for continued loving structure and guidance by the adults they have learned to trust. Along with guidance, they need enough freedom mixed in for them to explore their world with greater responsibility for their decisions and actions. Adding to the difficulty of the age is the incredible pressures placed on them by modern culture, to be adult before their time. Youth ministry is a vitally important aspect of a local church, requiring unique gifting to be effective.

If a young person has not given their life to Christ by age 21, the likelihood of them doing so is about 1 in 100. The most important time for young people to give their lives to Christ is in the Junior High and High School years. Thus, a youth ministry can be very important and a stabilizing factor within the church. This book cannot begin to address in detail the dynamics of youth ministry. Only a few principles are shared here, which are helpful for those providing for educational services to the youth ministry or for church leadership to be able to adequately evaluate youth ministry. Some of the primary principles follow.

The most important skill to learn to be effective in ministry to youth is to build **relationships**. I remember when I was first involved in Youth for Christ ministry in San Diego. I was taught over and over again that winning didn't matter in games. My ability to teach was not all that important. The most important thing for me to do was to build a trusting, honest relationship with the young people that I was ministering to. This lesson did not come easy for me. I had been a very competitive athlete at a top level for several years. Winning was everything to me. One day my director and some kids I was discipling went out for a game of racquetball. As per usual for me, I played hard, which was fine. The problem this day was that one of the teens we were playing was very good, and my co-director, who was on my team, was very poor. The game was close, and I lost my temper more than once in attempting to win the game in spite of my teammate. When we won the game (barely) I was elated. Unfortunately, the other teens were unimpressed, and my partner was embarrassed and angry…with me! His undressing of me after the teens had gone home, reminding me of my purpose for ministry (that is, relationship is first) left an indelible impression on me.

Teenagers can tell a phony from 100 yards. Leaders must remember that whoever is involved in youth ministry must have an ability to build relationships, to be socially proactive, able to bond with young people. Of course, a youth leader should be someone of maturity with high energy, as youth ministry is not meant for the timid at heart.

The second principle is that of **balance**. In Luke 2:52 the Word of God says that, *"Jesus grew in wisdom and in knowledge and in favor with God and man."* Again, referring back to Youth For Christ, they discuss very openly their philosophy of ministry, which is called, "The Balanced Life Philosophy." This simply means that human beings need to grow in every major area of life, intellectually, socially, relationally and spiritually. (Or mentally, physically, emotionally and spiritually). If one is so spiritually minded they will become no earthly good, or if someone is totally involved in the physical aspect of growth they can limit themselves and their future potential.

Thus, balance is necessary. So is balance necessary in the programming that one provides for young people. There should be a balance of physical, social, intellectual and especially spiritual activities.

A third principle is **family**. Young people have a significant amount of loyalty to his or her family of origin. This loyalty will continue throughout the majority of their life. Thus, they need guidance from their parents, yet often, their parents are inaccessible or difficult at best for the young person to talk with. A youth minister and the youth ministry can be strategic helpers for needs not easily met by the family. Having some basic knowledge of the family structure that the individual child comes from can be important for youth ministry.

One of the greatest mistakes frequently made in youth ministries occurs when the youth minister or the ministry itself functions completely contrary or secretively in relationship to the family. It's important to include the family where possible. Having family days, or activities with Father/Son, Mother/Daughter, Mother/Son, Father/Daughter, can be a very effective and important ways of integrating the whole family into the overall ministry of the church. Complete isolation of youth ministry from the main stream of church life is certainly not desirable. In fact, a goal should be to integrate the young person into the church so that they can continue to function in areas of leadership when no longer a youth. This is best done through having young people involved in the programs of the church such as Sunday school teaching, evangelism, helps ministry, worship, etc., on a regular and systematic basis.

Finally, it is strongly recommended that a leader review the effective youth ministry programs within the city that they serve. **Joining** with such ministries as Youth For Christ, Campus Crusade For Christ, or very effective local church ministries can be most judicious. Do not try and do everything yourself. It is best to network with other youth ministries so that a well-rounded program, which is cost and time effective can be developed. There's absolutely no reason to re-create the wheel. Wherever possible, hang onto the coat tails of other successful ministries. In fact, it will assist the church in the successful development of youth ministry.

For more on adolescents and their unique needs, I would strongly recommend Dr. Bohac's book Human Development. This book covers development from pre-natal through adulthood. Especially note the section on the growth and development of youth. It is a very important study. Dr. Bohac's book is listed in the bibliography for reference purposes.

"If a man empties his purse into his head no one can take it away from him. An investment in knowledge always pays the best interest."

Benjamin Franklin, Poor Richards Almanac

Chapter 13

Adults and Discipleship

The very best models found within scripture for the education of children, youth and adults is found in the Old Testament, as demonstrated in the lifestyle of the Hebrews, and also in the New Testament as modeled by the ministries of Jesus and the Apostle Paul. Reviewed here are some of the reasons for discipleship and the subsequent goals of teaching. The purpose of which is to present to the education leader the importance of a solid adult educational ministry within the local church.

As discussed in the second chapter, one fairly clear Old Testament picture of the importance of the teaching ministry for adults is found in the life of Ezra.

Ezra was a scribe who eventually became a judge in Israel. He was also a priest, raised in Babylonian captivity, but was one of the primary leaders, both political and spiritual, of the revival or restoration of the Children of Israel back to their homeland.

The reader is reminded that in the tenth verse of chapter 7 in the book of Ezra it says, *"Ezra had set his heart to study the law of the Lord and to practice it and to teach his statues and ordinances in Israel."* Ezra is a type or presents a picture of someone who is dedicated to the educational ministry. He had set his heart to study the law of the Lord, to study the Torah or the five books of Moses and the history of Israel. To study meant to meditate consistently and actively on God's Word. It included to dialog about it with his friends until he had the entire story of the Old Testament memorized.

Secondly, he studied the word of God for the purpose of practicing it. The word practice in the Hebrew means to practice godliness, or to follow the precepts learned from scriptural study. But it further means to practice the ministry as God had called him to. So he began to practice his teaching and priestly ministry long before he had the opportunity to do so in Israel.

The ultimate goal of Ezra (and of our training) was to teach. In Ezra's case, he desired to teach in Israel. Our goals may be a bit less ambitious. It is in the book of Nehemiah, chapter 8, that the fulfillment of the goal of Ezra is recorded.

This gives us a fairly clear picture of the important role of the teacher in the Old Testament. That role was to study and thoroughly know God's Word, then to apply it to ones' life, becoming skilled in the areas of ministry, whether the priesthood, prophet or scribe. Finally, the goal of being able to impart to a large group of people all that the teacher, in this case Ezra, had learned during his time of study was paramount.

Over the years of biblical history many things changed but the primary role of the teacher in the Hebrew community did not significantly change. In some ways the setting changed from the temple to local synagogues, but for the most part the teaching ministry was seen as vital, important, necessary and the primary mode of transmitting the truth of God's Word to his people.

When Jesus began his ministry, the people of God were in a time of transition, under the occupation of the Roman government. They were a hungry people, seeking for answers to life; seeking for a Messiah. The teaching ministry in the Old Testament, the Talmud or the Commentaries on the Hebrew scriptures had been developed over many years and there was great importance given to the teaching ministry. When Jesus came on the scene, he came primarily as a teacher.

In the book of St. John, chapter 3, Nicodemus came to visit Jesus by night. He made a proclamation that was shared broadly by people within the community, that Jesus was a Rabbi or a teacher. In John chapter 3:2, it states *"this man came to him,* (meaning Nicodemus) *by night and said to him, 'Rabbi we know that you have come from*

God as a teacher. For no one can do these signs that you do unless God is with him.'"

Jesus began to expound on the kingdom of God from the beginning of his ministry. Jesus' focus of ministry has been described by many as a healing or deliverance ministry. But ultimately, when reviewing the totality of scripture, it becomes apparent that Jesus' primary focus was teaching. Signs and wonders followed the teaching of the Word. His primary audience for his teaching ministry was first and foremost, the twelve apostles. They received the direct teaching, the clear revelation of who he was, what God's Word was about, and what God's plan was for all mankind.

Secondly the seventy, then upwards of 500 and eventually the multitudes heard his teaching. They did not receive the detailed plan that was received by the apostles. Thus, when Jesus gave his Great Commission in Matthew 28 to his apostles (at this point the eleven apostles), he made a very clear and important statement. In the sixteenth verse of chapter 28 it says,

> *"But the eleven disciples proceeded to Galilee to the mountain which Jesus had designated. When they saw Him, they worshipped Him. But some were doubtful. And Jesus came up and spoke to them saying, 'All authority has been given to me in heaven and on earth, go therefore and make disciples of all the nations. Baptizing them in the name of the Father, and the Son and the Holy Spirit. Teaching them to observe all that I commanded you and lo, I am with you always, even to the end of the age.'"*

Many theologians would say that this was a summary of the most cogent points Jesus made after his resurrection and before his ascension. Clearly, Jesus is giving a mandate to his apostles and the church receives this mandate as individual believers. Thus, the primary focus of ministry should be the making of disciples of all people groups.

A disciple is one who sits at the feet of a master teacher. One who is willing to submit themselves to a learning and growing process.

Along with that comes baptism or the willingness to die to ones' old life and completely submit themselves to a new life of teaching and training. Of course, what the disciples were to be taught was everything that they had observed, everything they saw Jesus do, and everything that he commanded or taught.

This is still the Great Commission for us today. It is one of the most important reasons why the adult teaching ministry is needed. Teaching fulfills (at least in part) the commandment of our Lord. The Great Commission that he gave to all believers and to all the church, was a mandate to teach and train individuals to maturity in Christ. Another picture of this is found in the book of Ephesians, where Paul speaks about the gifts that were given by Christ to the earth. He states in the fourth chapter, beginning with the eleventh verse, *"And he gave some as apostles and some as prophets, some as evangelists, some as pastors and teachers, for the equipping of the saints, for the work of service for the building up of the Body of Christ. Until we all come into the unity of the faith and of the knowledge of the Son of God, to a mature man, to the measure of the stature which belongs to the fullness of Christ. As a result,* (in other words, the results of the teaching ministry will be) *we are no longer to be children, tossed here and there by waves and carried about by every wind of doctrine by the trickery of men, by craftiness and deceitful scheming. But speaking the truth in love, we are to grow up in all aspects into Him who is the head, even Christ. For whom the whole body being fitted and held together by that which every joint supplies according to the proper working of each individual part causes the growth of the body for the building up of itself in love."* In other words, the importance of the five-fold ministry and especially the teaching ministry is to equip the saints so that they can serve the Lord. This teaching ministry is to consistently continue until God's people come to the full knowledge of the Son of God, into the maturity that is required for one to stand firm in faith.

Thus, the teaching ministry was vital in the time of Christ and was the primary focus of ministry of His apostles. If this is the New

Testament pattern, should it not be followed today? Perhaps a few other pictures from the book of Acts will help strengthen my emphasis. For instance, after the great outpouring of the Holy Spirit on the day of Pentecost, Acts 2:37-38 says, *"Now when they heard this, they were pierced to the heart and said to Peter and the rest of the Apostles, 'brethren what shall we do?' Peter said to them, 'Repent and let each of you be baptized in the name of Jesus Christ for the forgiveness of your sins, and you shall receive the gift of the Holy Spirit.'"* Then verse 41 says, *"So then those who had received his word were baptized and there were added that day about three thousand souls and they were continually devoting themselves to the apostles teaching and to fellowship to the breaking of bread and to prayer."* In other words, they were developing a balanced spiritual life through the teaching ministry, which included fellowship with one another, through the breaking of bread or communion, as well as fellowship meals, and of course through prayer.

This occurred as a pattern, day by day. Verse 46 then says, *"And day by day continuing with one mind in the temple and breaking bread from house to house. They were taking their meals together with gladness and sincerity of heart, praising God and having favor with all the people. And the Lord was adding to their number day by day, those who were being saved."*

Thus, from the very beginning of the outpouring of the Holy Spirit, the teaching ministry was vitally important. What did the apostles teach? The apostles taught what they observed and everything that Jesus commanded. That is all that they knew. They had a clear picture of the revelation of who Jesus Christ is. Further, they had a full understanding of God's plan from the beginning of time to their present day. This is what they were commissioned to transmit by the preaching and teaching of the Word to those that were being saved. Thus, they taught them daily to grow in the things of God.

Now if one were to continue to read through the book of Acts, they would see other pictures that show the importance of the teaching ministry. In chapter 8 of the book of Acts there was a great scattering of the church because of the persecution of Stephen, and the adverse effects of Saul (who latter became Paul) in terms of his persecution of the church. Part of the remnant of the church in Jerusalem that was scattered ended up in Antioch.

> In Acts 11:19-26 it says, *"So then those who were scattered because of the persecution that arose in connection with Stephen, made their way to Phoenicia, and Cyprus, and Antioch, speaking the word to no one except to Jews alone, but there were some of them, men of Cyprus and Cyrene who came to Antioch to begin speaking to the Greeks also. Preaching the Lord Jesus. And the hand of the Lord was with them and a large number who believed, turned to the Lord. And the news about them reached the ears of the church at Jerusalem and they sent Barnabas off to Antioch. And when they had come and witnessed the grace of God, he rejoiced and began to encourage all with resolute heart to remain true to the Lord for he was a good man, full of the Holy Spirit and faith. And considerable numbers were brought to the Lord. He left for Tarsus to look for Saul. When he had found him, he brought him to Antioch. (This is the key part) And it came about that for an entire year they met with the church and taught considerable numbers and the disciples where first called Christians at Antioch."*

Thus the effect of the teaching ministry in Antioch, under the anointing of the Holy Spirit working through Barnabas and Saul, was a transmission of the very life of Christ into them, and they became as it were, little Christ's. Everyone in the city recognized them as people who carried that same basic lifestyle that Christ did. Thus, showing again the importance of the teaching ministry.

> A final picture can be seen in Acts 19:8-11, which says, *"And he entered the Synagogue and continued speaking out boldly for three months, reasoning and persuading them about the kingdom of God. But when some were becoming hardened, disobedient, speaking evil of the way before the multitude, he withdrew from them and took away the disciples, reasoning daily in the school of Tyrannus (A*

rented schoolroom). This took place for two years so that all who lived in Asia heard the word of the Lord both Jews and Greeks. And God was performing extraordinary miracles by the hands of Paul."

The result of the teaching was a tremendous spreading of the Gospel through the disciples that were being trained.

Paul was an outstanding and yet a very systematic teacher. He would have learned his basic teaching style the same way that Ezra did. He was a man that had set his heart to know the law. He was a Jew's Jew. He was a teacher of the Hebrew faith, prior to his conversion on the Damascus road.

When He taught, He would have taught everything taught within the scriptures in light of the cross. He would have taught systematically, clearly and consistently. He would have had His students asking questions and grappling with the concepts of the Word of God until a revelation of truth became theirs.

It is through that process, systematic teaching, that one can make disciples within the local church. Thus, the New Testament model of the church found both at Antioch and Ephesus should be the model for today. (For further insights on this subject matter please see, *"Supernatural Architecture,"* by Dr. DeKoven).

Mentoring to Maturity:
The Secret to Successful Education

Home school education is a modern revisitation of the biblical model of training in which the training and education of children was done primarily in the home. Specialized relationships can and often do develop between parent and child, parent and children or in other small class environments. Unfortunately, this dynamic intimate process that is developed through the home school of Christian school environment usually ends upon completion of formal education. If indeed special intimacy and character transfer (the "catching" of various habits, attitudes, etc.) does occur as demonstrated through small group interaction (both positive and negative transfer), why not continue it throughout one's life time? Is it possible to continue this close intimate relationship when the young man or woman has completed "formal" education and is tasked to take one's place in the larger society (even the church)?

Human Development

As a teenager matures, it is natural for him/her to develop a certain amount of his or her own identity, goals and purposes. For the great majority, this process of moving from child to adult is fairly smooth. Naturally our children will not see the world exactly as we do (who does?), but hopefully their personal faith will lead them to embrace Christ, his word and his church. This process of culturalization should have been in process for many years. The hope is that they will continue to embrace the "faith of their fathers" as they seek their place in the world, the church and move towards satisfying their need for emotional intimacy. The seeds for the successful transition that is hoped for may be in the continuation and formalization of a dynamic process experienced in home schooling and other small group processes (home fellowship, cell churches, small private schools, etc.).

The Jesus Model

It is apparent that Jesus valued all the family, as he willingly and effectively ministered to all segments of family life. However, it does not take but a limited study of the gospels to see that Jesus' primary focus was on the training, equipping, empowering, and releasing of his chosen disciples to be and do all they saw him do. (Matthew 28:18-20).

What is a Disciple?

A disciple is one who simply and obediently follows Jesus. He/she is a person who has freely chosen to enter into a relationship with Christ and his church, whereby a new pattern of living or life style is developed over time, conforming to the image of Christ. (I Corinthians 11:7). The long-term goal of this specialized relationship is to bring the disciple to full maturity (Ephesians 4:13) and thus fulfill the purpose of God for their life as directed by the Holy Spirit. Discipleship is not an option for the believer.

The Place of Discipleship

True discipleship is best called mentorship. A mentor is defined as "a wise and trusted teacher" (Funk and Wagnall's). Parents are special mentors, as are spiritual leaders in a local church. Jesus was not limited to physical locations, but in fact mentored or discipled his followers wherever he was. He often used the natural world to illustrate points (lilies of the valley, whited sepulchers) with a focus on transmitting both teaching and life in the process.

Today, there are many models for discipleship that have been developed. Most are strong on doctrine, some on character, but few contain the unique components of total discipleship that were modeled by Christ. First the traditional model.

Types of Discipleship

The most common type of discipleship is one based upon the learning of the basic doctrines of the church, as presented in Hebrews 5:11-6:3. These doctrines are foundational to the faith and are generally presented within a local church subsequent to individual salvation. This is often a positive beginning, but usually ends the discipleship process. The assumption is that once a person has received doctrinal teaching that growth in spiritual life will continue unabated and smooth throughout church life. This is no doubt true for some, but woefully inadequate for a great majority. This model is similar to the catechism model found in many liturgical church systems. These are usually taught by "professional clergy" or highly trained lay leaders.

The second system is less formal and focuses on layman to layman instruction. This program is also time limited, and usually focuses on a combination of doctrine and character. The most positive aspect to this is the greater number of potential disciplers ministering to disciples and the removal of potential hindrances to clergy/layman conflict. Some people are intimidated by clergy as instructors. The obvious weaknesses include the level of training of the discipler and again the time limited nature of the process (usually a few weeks to several months).

Discipleship Model-Mentorship

A more effective way of discipling and transitioning the young person to adult maturity and the adult convert to fullness in Christ occurs through a mentorship process. Most everyone needs a father/mother figure who can individually assist a believer through the growth process. That process has three characteristics as described in Allen Curry's article in *The Christian Educators Journal* on **Adult Education.** They are:

1. Leading people to follow Jesus and to pattern their lives after his
2. Providing personal examples of what it means to be like Jesus, and
3. Designing a church context for fostering discipleship.

It begins with follow-up, continues with reproduction, then equipping, releasing and leading. Let me describe each here and relate it to mentorship and discipleship.

Following

Following is designed to ensure that the initial commitment made by a new convert is true. It lays foundations for belief and hopefully introduces them to the security of the life of the church. This process should produce intimacy with Christ as a first stage of development (see Journey to Wholeness: Restoration of the Soul by Dr. DeKoven).

Reproducing

Reproducing is the process of encouraging the new believer to share his or her faith with their sphere of influence. Of course, this is a primary way of introducing the gospel to those in need. Thus, training in evangelism is usually a part of the discipleship/training process. These first two segments are usually the entirety of the discipleship in standard programs.

Equipping

Equipping the saints for the work of service is the primary responsibility for church leadership of the five-fold ministry (Ephesians 4:11). The equipping process is usually presented in two fashions. First is the standard church programs including Adult Sunday school, singles ministries, etc. The second is to send the best of the students to a regional or national Bible College, where the most committed potential leadership is referred to for formal training and education. The strength of these schools includes academic resources (library, computers, professors, etc.) and the learning environment. The weakness is the loss of experiencing the primary leadership of the local church, and being away from the dynamic life of the local church for one to four years. For the great majority, they never return to the local church from which they came, or are untrainable when they return (they think they know more than the local leadership). Reintegrating into the local church vision after a four or more-year absence can be most difficult. True equipping that leads to release into the gifting of God and eventual leadership is best found in the dynamic of local church life. A mentorship process, which should be both formal and informal, is needed to equip the saints for full service in the Kingdom of God.

Mentoring—Adult Education

Mentoring combines the key ingredients for effective adult education. This includes:

1. Modeling or the learning process through observing and interacting with other adults which will encourage accountability and growth.
2. Systematic instruction of major theological and biblical subjects combined with practical application for ones' life

and service. There is need for immediacy of application for the adult learner.

From basic faith development through full leadership training, the method of Christ and thus the appropriate model for the church is discipleship/mentorship. The church is tasked to provide for education and training from birth to grave. This is best done in small group, home based education under the supervision of the local church.

A Final Thought on Mentorship

In 1 John 2: 12-14, the Apostle writes; *"I am writing to you little children, because your sins are forgiven you for his name's sake. I am writing to you fathers because you know him who has been from the beginning. I am writing to you young men because you have overcome the evil one. I have written to you children because you know the Father. I have written to you fathers because you know him who is from the beginning. I have written you young men because you are strong and the Word of God abides in you, and you have overcome the evil one."*

The Apostle outlines for us the three phases of spiritual development. All three (children, young men and fathers) require mentorship, wise teachers to lift the novice or even the warrior to a higher level of commitment to Christ. However, as long as we are in the Lord, we will always be on a journey to be all God created us to be. We must remember Paul's prayer, *"that I may know him…"*. Paul's mentor was Christ himself. May we all grow from glory unto glory until we reach the fullness of our destiny in Christ.

The Modern Church

In the present hour there are a number of different ways to develop adult education programs. In liturgically oriented churches one can find a form of catechism which begins early in a young persons' life and continues through adulthood. This form of confirmation or conformational system is the training system of the teaching ministry.

As adults, they primarily receive their education in a Sunday school class or perhaps in a home fellowship. Unfortunately, there has not been a significant emphasis on teaching and therefore, there is a lack of clear biblical understanding. In fact, some have said that the church in America is biblically illiterate. That is, they really do not know what the Word of God is all about and how to apply it to their life. Thus, there is a need for more than just a simple Sunday school class or home fellowship.

One cannot rely upon Sunday morning or the Sunday evening service alone to instruct people towards maturity. All adults should be fully trained and equipped to do their part in the kingdom of God.

This is especially true in light of God's mandate to bring his people to a place of maturity and to fully disciple whole nations or ethnic groups. Thus, there is a need for systematic training programs across the entire spectrum of Church endeavors in this generation. In response to this acute need, many churches have established complete Bible college programs or training institutes within their local assembly.

There are many excellent ministries that presently exist that can assist local churches to develop a comprehensive adult education program. Many are highly effective in releasing people into areas of gifting and calling. What should the components of a good adult education program include?

First of all, there needs to be a course or courses in basic doctrine. That is, to understand the foundational principles of our faith as discussed in Hebrews 6. The foundational doctrines of faith include, baptism, salvation, who God is, who Christ is, who the Holy Spirit is, etc. Further, what are the gifts of the Holy Spirit, what is a Christian family like? How do I handle my finances? This is basic teaching that can be found in most books for new converts.

Secondly, there needs to be instruction in the area of godly character. That is, there needs to be an emphasis within the teaching program of conforming ones will to the will of God as found within the Word of God. The only way to do this is to challenge adult believers to look into the mirror of truth found within the scriptures with a willingness to change through the process of repentance or a change of thinking which leads to a change of lifestyle. Solomon said it like this, *"As he* (a man) *thinks in his heart, so is he,"* (Proverbs 23:7). The apostle Paul added,

> *"And be not conformed to this world: but be ye transformed by the renewing of your mind, that ye may prove what is that good, and acceptable, and perfect, will of God,"* (Romans 12:2).

Thus, one must be confronted with issues of sin through the teaching ministry. The best time to do so is when a new convert is young in the Lord.

It is best not to wait until they have learned to develop religious defenses to protect them from the "onslaught of God's Word." In reality, there are many callused, hardened saints of God who are that way because they have been hurt from past church relationships and have become unwilling to open their heart to the Word of God. When a new convert enters the church, they are open and teachable. It is fairly easy to work with them individually or in small groups, and thus make a powerful impact on their life. It is in the beginning of their walk with God, learning the fundamentals, when it is possible to work through the problem areas of life and come to a place of maturity and wholeness in God.

Third, adults need to be taught areas of practical ministry. That is, things like how the gifts of the Holy Spirit work, how to study the Word effectively, and the dynamics of the Christian life. Further, courses which deal with doctrinal and theological topics such as angels and demons and to answer questions such as what do all these words mean that are used within the Christian church, like salvation, justification, sanctification, and propitiation, mean? Other topics include, "How is one supposed to treat their neighbors? What is evangelism and how does one learn to evangelize?" All these topics and many more are germane for the adult learner.

These systematic courses offered within the local church structure are readily available and most powerful. An adult education program helps set the stage for the equipping and releasing of men and women into full service within the local church and beyond. Also, as the Holy Spirit begins to move on someone's life, it may release him or her into greater areas of service. Often, evangelists, teachers, pastors, prophets and apostles are raised up within the local church and released from that community of faith, always keeping a tie to the mother church, which is again a New Testament pattern seen in the book of Acts through the ministry of the Apostle Paul.

Adult education is vital as is all areas of education within the church. One cannot emphasize enough the importance of it. It was important in the life of Moses. He (through his scribe) wrote down all the things that had occurred from creation until the time he went home to be with the Lord. All throughout the Old Testament scribes wrote down the important events inspired by the Holy Spirit, which are known as the Old Testament scriptures. In the New Testament, the pattern of the life of Christ, seen in his teaching of children, where he blessed them, nurturing them all the way through adulthood, is evident. He ministered both practically as well as instructionally to bring about the purposes of God.

In the life of Peter and Paul, as with all the apostles, the same basic program of teaching and training, equipping people for further service is seen. Throughout church history one can observe the importance of teaching to impart the truth of who Jesus Christ is to the whosoever will that may come into the house of the Lord. In these days, God is building his kingdom. But he builds his kingdom foundationally, line upon line, precept upon precept. He wants to build it strong, with a firm and solid foundation. That foundation can be positively and powerfully laid through the teaching ministry that is systematic and comprehensive. It should be found in and through the local church.

Bibliography

1. Bohac, Joseph J. *Human Development: A Christian Perspective*, Vision Publishing, Ramona, CA, 1994

2. Byrne, H.W. *A Christian Approach to Education*, Mott Media, Milford, MI, 1977

3. Clark, R.E., Brubaker, J., and Zuck, R.B.; *Childhood Education in the Church*, Moody Press, Chicago, Ill. 1986

4. Crain, William, *Theories of Development, 3rd Edition*, Prentice-Hall, N.J., 1992.

5. DeKoven, Stan E., *Keys to Successful Living*, Vision Publishing, Ramona, CA, 1996

6. _____. *Journey to Wholeness: Restoration of the Soul*, Vision Publishing, Ramona, CA 1992

7. _____. *Supernatural Architecture: Building the Church of the 21st Century*, Wagner Institute Publishing, Colorado Springs, CO 1999

8. Edge, Findley B., T*eaching for Results*, Broadman and Holman, Nashville, TN 1996

9. Ford, L., *A Curriculum Design Manual for Theological Education*, Broadman Press, Nashville, TN, 1991

10. Kienel, Paul A. Ed., *Philosophy of Christian School Education*, ACSI Press, Colorado Springs, CO 1978

11. Lopez, Diane, *Teaching Children*, Crossway Books, Wheaton, IL, 1988.

12. Peterson, Michael L. *Philosophy of Education*, Intervarsity Press, Downers Grove, IL, 1986

13. Stein, Robert H. *The Method and Message of Jesus' Teaching*, Westminster John Knox Press, Louisville, KY, 1994

14. Wilhoit, J. and Ryken, L., *Effective Bible Teaching*, Baker Book House, Grand Rapids, MI, 1988.

15. Virkler, Mark, *Teaching for Transformation*, Communion with God Press, Elma, NY, 1990

Appendices

APPENDIX 1

Teacher's Resolutions

I Resolve:

1. To love my pupils more and show that love in thoughtful ways.
2. To pray daily for my pupils.
3. To spend more time in preparation and Bible study.
4. To be regular and punctual, notifying the departmental or general superintendent as soon as possible when it is necessary to be absent.
5. To follow up absentees and report on the follow-up.
6. To call on the homes of all my pupils once this year.
7. To attend monthly staff meetings regularly and with helpful suggestions.
8. To take part in the social activities of my class or department, realizing that "a merry heart does good like a medicine."
9. To have a specific aim for the lesson each week and evaluate results.
10. To encourage pupil participation in class discussion and activities.
11. To emphasize missions as well as evangelism in my teaching.
12. To strive to live out the truths I teach to others.
13. To be accurate in record keeping.
14. To be present at least fifteen minutes before the Sunday school opens.
15. To greet my pupils with a friendly smile and disposition.
16. To cooperate with the general superintendent as well as the other teachers and officers of the Sunday school.
17. To keep my life clean according to the standards of God's Word.

18. To attend the regular services of the church and train my pupils to be present.
19. To develop and maintain the highest possible standards of administrative and teaching efficiency.
20. To depend upon the Holy Spirit for definite guidance in my preparation and teaching of the lesson.

APPENDIX 2

The Teacher's Covenant

As a Christian teacher, I appreciate the privilege I have in engaging in this high and holy calling according to the word. "And they that be wise (teachers) shall shine (righteousness) as the stars forever and ever." (Daniel 12:3)

Depending upon God, I humbly and earnestly pledge myself to the following standard, which our school has adopted, believing it to be in accordance with His plan.

1. I will at all times manifest a deep concern spiritually for the welfare of the members of my class. My first desire shall be to bring about the salvation of each pupil who does not know the Lord Jesus Christ, and to encourage the spiritual growth of those who do. I will carefully prepare my lesson and make each class session a matter of earnest prayer. (Isaiah 54:13).
2. I will endeavor to lead all my pupils to attain a high standard of regular attendance, punctuality, bringing Bible, preparation of lesson, giving offerings, and staying for morning worship. (Hebrews 10:24, 25).
3. I will attend our Sunday morning and evening services and use my influence to urge the members of my class to be present, realizing that Sunday school and church are inseparable. I will lend my support to the mid-week services of my church and endeavor to attend at least one service. (Hebrews 10:24, 25).
4. As a member of the church, I will teach in accordance with its doctrines and will set an example in dress, conversation, Christian deportment, and prayer. (I Timothy 4:12; I Timothy 3:1-6).

5. If at any time, through sickness or other emergency, I am unable to teach my class, I will notify my Supervisor at the earliest possible moment. (I Corinthians 4:2).
6. I understand that it is my responsibility to see that all absentees in my class are contacted to ensure their health and welfare. I will strive to visit the home of each pupil at least once every year. (Matthew 18:2).
7. As a Christian teacher, I will attend, unless unavoidably hindered, the worker's conferences and worker's training class offered by my church school. If no training is provided, I will study privately at least one textbook a year. (I Timothy 2:15).
8. At the worker's conference I will submit a report of my class as may be required by the Supervisor. (Luke 16:2).

APPENDIX 3

Ten Commandments For Teachers

1. Thou shalt have no selfish pleasure before thy duty to thy class.
2. Thou shalt not make unto thee any personal engagement, or any trifling excuse for being away from thy class. Thou shalt not bow down thyself to questionable amusements or to any conduct unworthy of the emulation of the pupils.
3. Thou shalt not take the responsibility of a class in vain, for the Lord thy God will hold him or her guilty who taketh <u>Lightly</u> a God-given task.
4. Remember thy class to keep it whole.
5. Honor the calling and thy class, that thy days may be long in the success which the Lord thy God giveth thee.
6. Thou shalt not kill thy pupil's interest by thine irregular attendance.
7. Thou shalt be sure in thy faith in the Word of God and in thine interpretation of it in word and deed.
8. Thou shalt not steal the time of thy class and the peace of mind of your supervisor by being tardy.
9. Thou shalt not bear false witness by failing to practice what thou teachest.
10. Thou shalt not covet superficial success, but only that which results from careful and prayerful preparation.

APPENDIX 4

The Teacher's Psalm

The Lord is my helper, I shall not fear in guiding these pupils.

He leadeth me into the Holy of Holies before I prepare this lesson.

He leadeth me to the heart of the truth, and prepareth the minds of the pupils for the truth.

He giveth me a vision of the immortality of these lives.

He leadeth me to see the sacredness of teaching His Book,

Yea, though I become discouraged and despair at times, yet shall I lift up my head, for His promises cannot fail me.

His Word will not return to Him void, and my faith undimmed shall burn through all the coming years.

Thou walketh before me that the seed planted shall grow.

Thou shall stand by my side on Sunday, and speak through these lips so that pupils feel the nearness of God.

Thou shalt cause each broken effort to gather sheaves through unnumbered years. My joy is full when I know that every effort in Thy name shall abide forever.

Surely Thy love and watchcare shall be with me every day of my life, and some day I shall live with those who turn many to righteousness for ever and ever.

Rosalee Mills Appleby

APPENDIX 5

Seventy Ways To Teach A Sunday School Lesson
Adapted from R. Bryant Mitchell

1.	BLACKBOARD	Drawings, handwork may be displayed on board.
2.	BULLETIN BOARD	Use cork, fiber or monks cloth adjusted to children's height. Display news clippings, drawings and prize lessons.
3.	DIAGRAMS AND OUTLINES	
4.	FLANNELGRAPH	Pin on bulletin board or use separate stand.
5.	FLASH CARDS	Purchased or homemade.
6.	GOSPEL CARTOONS	From newspapers, magazines, and Sunday School papers.
7.	MAPS AND CHARTS	Flat and roll sets available - Draw on blackboard.
8.	POSTERS	Collect for class use - Make it a student project.
9.	SAND TABLE	Keep clean, closed and locked between classes.
II.	**GROUP PARTICIPATION**	
10.	CHORAL READING	Good for visual understanding, pronunciation and vocalizing.
11.	CLASS DISCUSSION	Very helpful under teacher's guidance.
12.	CLASS PLANNING	Plan activities, projects, lessons together.

13.	DEBATE	Plan ahead, choose debaters, coaching by teacher.
14.	PANEL DISCUSSION	Plan ahead with selected panel.
15.	READING IN TURN	Gives individual participation for each one.
16.	SMALL GROUP DISCUSSION	Divide class into groups of three or four with leader. Assemble all groups for a total class discussion.
17.	STUDENT LEADERSHIP	Train students for executive and detailed class leadership.
18.	SOLVING PROBLEMS	Relate lessons to contemporary problems. Teacher guides in selecting Christian answers.
19.	UNITED PRAYER	Recite the Lord's prayer every Sunday. Special prayer sessions for missions, the church, needy pupils, classmates, world conditions, salvation of unsaved loved ones.

III. VISUAL AIDS

20.	MOVIES	Some free, some rental. Obtain through superintendent or pastor.
21.	PHOTOGRAPHS	From picture magazines, circulate from city library.

IV. QUIZ METHODS

22.	CATECHISM	Well proven scriptural method, graded courses available.
23.	MEMORY DRILL	Young folks enjoy competition and learn much.
24.	QUESTIONS AND ANSWER	Divide class, each side prepares questions for the other - teacher prepared questions.

V. CLASS ACTIVITIES

25.	BIBLE GAMES	Special books or game packets available. Integrate with lesson.

26.	BUILDING PROJECTS	
27.	CLASS PROJECTS	Prepare flannel graphs, make diagram of tabernacle, maps & charts.
28.	CLASS TRIPS	To museum, missionary display, visiting exhibits, special speakers, directed play. Especially helpful for younger children.
29.	GROUP GAMES	Physical for small children, mental for older children. Relate to lesson.
30.	HANDCRAFT	Paper scissors and glue - clay, modeling, plaster, decorating mottoes, soap, woodcarving, picture coloring, etc.
31.	VISITATION AND EVANGELISM	Visit hospitals, shut-ins, absentees, distribute tracts, witnessing teams.
32.	WRITING	Essays, lesson quizzes, Sunday school newspaper.

VI. MUSIC

33.	MUSIC	Vocal and instrumental group numbers, class singing.
34.	CASSETTES AND CD's	Children can bring appropriate music for lesson background and for music instruction.
35.	RECORDINGS	Available from publisher; make your own; copy from radio; TV or record player. Good for Bible story telling and sound effects.
36.	TV and RADIO	Copy on recorder from significant broadcasts.

VII. OBJECT LESSONS

37.	BIBLE TRAVEL GAMES	Illustrated map of lesson locations.
38.	DISPLAYS	Missionary exhibit, Bible land objects.

39.	HANDIWORK	
40.	MAKE IT YOURSELF	Common household articles
41.	MODELS	The Temple, the Tabernacle, Noah's Ark.
42.	PLASTER WORK	Plaster of Paris or casting plaster, sets in 20 minutes. Plastic molds available or make molds of clay and cast.
43.	PUPPETS	Homemade or store bought. Illustrate Bible drama.
44.	PUZZLES	Purchase from supply store.

VIII. DRAMAS

45.	CHARACTER	Simple props only, imagination PERSONIFICATION will fill in blanks.
46.	DRAMATIZATION OF STORIES	Best not to memorize. Students learn story well and ad lib with guidance.
47.	IMAGINATIVE STORY TELLING	Records and tapes available for patterns. Use students.
48.	RADIO PRESENTATION	Let class make simulated radio broadcast.

IX. INDIVIDUAL STUDENT ACTIVITIES

49.	CLASS ASSIGNMENTS	
50.	CLASS RECITATION	Teachers assign a verse or paragraph and everyone recites each Sunday.
51.	CLASS WRITING	Fill in workbook or answers to questions in lesson.
52.	INDIVIDUAL RESEARCH	Teacher assigns special study in line with individual interests related to lesson, e.g. archeology, Bible and science, current events.

53.	INTERVIEWS WITH TEACHER	Keep informal and friendly.
54.	LESSON NOTEBOOK	Either scrapbook or loose leaf in addition to quarterly. Reward excellent work.
55.	PERSONAL COUNSELING	Formal appointment methods not good. Use casual, "Just happened to mention it" approach. Look for opportunity "breaks."
56.	PERSONAL PRAYER	Help students to develop personal prayer life. Lead in class and Sunday school prayer.
57.	REPORTS	Class activities and statistics, lesson findings.
58.	SCRAPBOOK	Developed by students
59.	SCRIPTURE MEMORY	Splendid courses available, Golden Text, Ten Commandments, Books of the Bible, Tribes of Israel, Scripture portions, etc.
60.	TEXTBOOK STUDY	From Sunday school or City Library, special projects.
61.	WORK BOOKS	Available with lesson or may be copied.

X. **TEACHER CENTERED PRESENTATION**

62.	BIOGRAPHICAL APPROACH	Character centered lessons.
63.	LECTURE	The most common form used and often the most dull. Spice it up with seventy-six other methods.
64.	PERSONAL EXAMPLE	The character and experiences of the teacher say as much as a lecture.
65.	PRESENTATION OF LESSON	Use simple well-planned outline. Stress only 2 or 3 main points.

66. REVIEW	Review, review, review. Relate series of lessons by review on last lesson.
67. SPIRITUAL ADMONITION	Apply spiritual truths; correct false impressions; apply Bible doctrines; relate scriptural teachings to modern problems; encourage individual participation. Occasional class consecration services are highly effective if not overdone.
68. STORY TELLING	Story CD's/DVD's available for teacher guidance. Use imagination. Do not overdo, minimize entertainment. Feature and emphasize spiritual application.
69. SURVEYS	Church and community statistics, national trends, spiritual needs, opportunities, accomplishments.
70. TESTIMONY	Both student and teacher's testimony very helpful. Bring in special people for testimony related to lessons. E.g. missionary, evangelist, Christian athlete, Christian nurse, Christian law enforcement officer, Christian businessman. Play tapes in lieu of personal appearance when necessary.

APPENDIX 6

Old Testament Road Map

This is a condensed Bible memory trip through the Old Testament. It should be learned in sections and then reviewed. The memory clues are not absolutely necessary but they do help in some cases. The teacher may put other events in the outline as he chooses. These are only a few of the basic high spots in the Old Testament.

How to use...Students should learn the content of each section. These include Creation, The Fall, etc. Then in a later review, the teacher instead of saying, e.g. the key term, "The Fall" may ask for the location of the "serpent in the garden", or the "forbidden fruit", or the "curse upon mankind". Any of these would come under Genesis 3, "The Fall". By this method the students learn much more of the Bible Story.

GENESIS	**CHAPTER**	**MEMORY CLUES**
Creation	1	
The Fall	3	
The Flood	7	(Seven Pairs)
Babel	11	(el)
Abraham	12	(12 tribes, Hebrews)
Sodom-Gomorrah	19	(fire, nine)
Isaac offered	22	(Two went)
Jacob wrestles	32	
Joseph in prison	40	(400 year captivity)

EXODUS	CHAPTER	MEMORY CLUES
(Egypt to Sinai)		
Bondage	1	
Burning Bush	3	
Bricks and straw	5	(B-r-i-c-k-5)
Ten plagues	10	
Passover	12	(Midnight)
Red Sea	14	
Ten Commandments	20	(Ten) X (Two tables)
Golden Calf	32	
Tabernacle finished	40	(Wanderings)

LEVITICUS	CHAPTER	MEMORY CLUES
Unclean beasts	11	
Moral laws	18	

NUMBERS	CHAPTER	MEMORY CLUES
(Sinai to Jordan, 40 years)		
Leave Sinai	10	
Spies report	13	
Water from the Rock	20	(Ex. Law from Rock)
Brazen serpent	21	

DEUTERONOMY	CHAPTER	MEMORY CLUES
(Repetition of the law)		
Ten Commandments	5	(10/12)
National Prophecies	28	

Moses buried	34	
JOSHUA	**CHAPTER**	**MEMORY CLUES**
(Promised Land)		
Cross Jordan	3	
Jericho falls	6	(six days, once)
Sun stand still	10	
JUDGES	**CHAPTER**	**MEMORY CLUES**
(Rule by Judges)		
Gideon	6	(sixth Judge)
Samson	13	(thirteenth Judge)
I SAMUEL	**CHAPTER**	**MEMORY CLUES**
(Samuel and Saul)		
Birth of Samuel	1	
Saul anointed King	10	(Ten toes)
David and Goliath	17	
I KINGS	**CHAPTER**	**MEMORY CLUES**
(Solomon to Ahaziah)		
(Elijah)		
Solomon's Wisdom	3	(2 women, 1 child)
Kingdom divided	12	(12 tribes)
Elijah and Ahab	18	(A eighteen)

II KINGS	CHAPTER	MEMORY CLUES
(Close of the Kingdom,		
Elisha)		
Elijah's mantle	2	(double portion)
Naaman the leper	5	(hand, 5 fingers)
Elisha's bones	13	
Ten tribes captivity	17	
I AND II CHRONICLES	(Repetition of Kings)	
EZRA AND NEHEMIAH	(Return to Jerusalem, Temple rebuilt.)	
ISAIAH	CHAPTER	MEMORY CLUES
(Messiah and the Kingdom)		
Virgin Birth	7	(Perfection)

APPENDIX 7

The Sunday School Assembly Programs

A. The opening Exercises.
   1. Call to order
      a. A small bell or start a song-anything to attract attention.
      b. Secure perfect order before starting.
   2. Song Service.
      a. Have several songs, choruses are better for children.
      b. Dead singing means a lifeless Sunday School.
      c. A good leader is important.
   3. Prayer and scripture reading.
   4. Special music and program.
      a. Good to have different classes represented from Sunday to Sunday.
   5. New Members.
   6. Superintendents instruction and announcements.
   7. Separation to classes.
      a. Best with music.
B. Closing Exercises
   1. Good song.
   2. Sunday School report.
      a. Honor classes.
      b. Emphasized Bibles-offering-attendance, etc...

3. Birthday offering.
   a. Song as they go forward.
   b. Prayer for the blessing of God throughout the next year.
   c. Song or verse.
   d. Some little remembrance should be given to each one.
4. Special number-memory work or class exercise.
5. Special talk by the pastor-superintendent or visiting speaker.
6. Closing song and benediction.

APPENDIX 8

Model VBS Program

Objectives - VBS is a summer program of Bible learning that lasts about three hours for five or ten days. It involves three segments: CLASSES, CRAFTS, and GAMES. The objective of VBS is to give children Bible oriented lessons and activities during the summer to help bridge the gap between Spring and Fall Sunday School. A lot of churches do not continue Sunday School throughout the summer, and without some kind of reinforcing activities, many children would tend to forget about God and church during summer. VBS is a good change of pace from regular Sunday School. The curriculum is different; it is more activity oriented. There are lots of music and singing; crafts to be done every day, and games and sports can be played outside. Every VBS ends with a mini-musicale for a closing program, so the children can show their friends and relatives some of the things they learned at VBS during the week.

Goals - The main goal of VBS is outreach. There are many children that do not go to Sunday School or to church. VBS is a fun, non-threatening place for children to come and learn about God. To be an efficient outreach program, there must be follow up. After VBS is over, postcards and other outreach materials must be sent regularly to the children, especially the unchurched ones. Also, invitations to attend Sunday School in the Fall must be extended.

I. PLANNING

    A. Pray

        1. Ask God for guidance

           a. Individually

           b. Staff meetings

        2. Pray for specific things

a. Teacher training
   b. That everyone will give his or her best
   c. Outreach ministry
   d. Wisdom and strength for leaders
  3. Get prayer partners
  4. Pray for VBS as a congregation
   a. During worship
  5. Pray at the end of VBS at evaluation/review meeting
B. Select curriculum
  1. VBS workshops
  2. Christian bookstores
  3. Information from publishers
C. Establish goals
  1. Unchurched outreach
  2. Sunday School enrollment for Fall
  3. All unchurched students will be contacted for follow-up
  4. Retention of materials by students
  5. Students will respond to Jesus in a new way because of VBS
D. Make a planning calendar
  1. 10 weeks before
   a. Attend VBS workshop
   b. Decide on curriculum
   c. Check out exam kit
   d. Publicity
   e. Planning session agenda

f. Begin recruiting staff members
2. 8 weeks before
   a. Have first general planning session
   b. Pass out teacher guides, teaching resources, craft books, and student books to teachers
3. 7 weeks before
   a. Plan pre-registration
   b. Plan details of publicity
   c. Check supplies and equipment
   d. Department Head planning session
4. 6 weeks before
   a. Publicity campaign
   b. Assign classrooms
   c. Have second general planning session
   d. Make sure all committees are functioning
   e. Order curriculum
5. 4 weeks before
   a. Begin pre-registration
   b. Have third general planning session
   c. Plan dedication service
   d. Pass curriculum out to teachers
6. 2 weeks before
   a. Plan agenda for Staff Evaluation meeting
   b. Hold Staff Dedication Day
   c. Check pre-registration and order extra curriculum if necessary

7. 1 week before
   a. Hold final planning session
   b. Prepare rooms and assembly area
8. During VBS
   a. Lead Staff devotions each day
   b. Prepare closing program letter and mail to all parents
   c. Check on plans for closing program
   d. Make final plans for Evaluation meeting
   e. Prepare attendance certificate for each student
   f. Prepare appreciation certificate for each staff member
   g If you want to give little gifts or plants to staff members, buy this week
9. 1 week after VBS
   a. Hold Evaluation meeting
   b. Complete all records
   c. Follow up all new converts and prospective Sunday School students
   d. Select next years VBS Coordinator
   e. Thank the staff for their hard work
   f. Thank God for successful VBS

II. BUDGETING

A. Check prices on all curriculum
   1. VBS Workshops
   2. Christian Bookstores
   3. From publishers

B. Check with previous years' Coordinator as to what was spent, and how many children were enrolled
   1. Read over Coordinators report
C. Check with the Christian Education Committee to find out what budget will be for VBS
D. Only order what is absolutely needed
   1. Many promotional materials can be made instead of purchased
   2. Check pre-registration numbers carefully and often
E. Take VBS offerings at Church
F. Take returnable leftover curriculum back to bookstore promptly for refund
G. Check leftover material from last year to see what can be used again

III. STAFF

A. You do not need more than about 19-20 people on the VBS staff.
   1. VBS Coordinator
   2. Assistant Coordinator
   3. Preschool teacher & helper
   4. Kindergarten teacher & helper
   5. Primary teacher & helper
   6. Middle grades teacher & helper
   7. Junior teacher & helper
   8. Craft leader
   9. Craft helpers
      a. Recruit Junior and Senior High students

10. Music director/pianist
11. Game leader
12. Game helpers
    a. Recruit Junior and Senior High students
13. Snack helpers
14. Supply coordinators
15. Baby-sitter
    a. Recruit Junior and Senior High students

IV. PUBLICITY
A. Distribute flyers and posters
   1. Churches
   2. Stores
      a. Grocery
      b. Christian bookstores
      c. Department stores
   3. Christian schools
   4. Laundromats
   5. Daycare centers
B. Newspaper ads
C. Radio spots
D. Answering machine
   1. Church
   2. Coordinator's
   3. Pastor's home
E. Skits

F. VBS photographs from last year in a display

G. Church newsletter

H. Play up pre-registration day in a big way

I. Sing VBS songs in the church

J. Slide presentations

K. Banners

L. Publicity aids from the VBS curriculum you choose

    1. Doorknob hangers

    2. Stationery

    3. Buttons

    4. T-shirts

    5. Postcards

    6. Balloons

    7. Theme bookmarks/stickers

    8. Bulletins/inserts

    9. Facebook page

V. FOLLOW-UP

A. Collect all leftover materials

    1. Store materials that can be used again next year

    2. Bring returnable curriculum back to Christian bookstore for refund

    3. Give non-returnable curriculum to missionaries if possible

B. Complete records

    1. Attendance list

    2. Staff list

    3. Financial record

4. Give names of new people to Pastor and the Evangelism/Outreach committee
5. Reports to other appropriate committees
6. Prepare a folder of pertinent information for the next year's coordinator

VI. SCHEDULE

	9:20-9:30	9:30-10:00	10:00-10:30	10:30-11:00	11:00-11:30	11:30-12:00
Preschool 2 & 3 yr. olds	opening	games (snack)	class	craft	class	closing
Kindergarten 4 & 5 yr. olds	opening	class	games (snack)	class	craft	closing
Primary 1st & 2nd grade	opening	craft	class	games (snack)	class	closing
Middle Grade 3rd & 4th grade	opening	class	craft	class	games (snack)	closing
Junior 5th & 6th grade	opening	class	craft	class	Games (snack)	closing

The Teaching Ministry of Dr. Stan DeKoven

Dr. Stan DeKoven is a licensed Marriage and Family Therapist, a Creative Life Coach and consults with individuals and churches nationally and internationally. Please visit his website for a complete list of seminars, or you may contact him at:

Dr. Stan DeKoven, President
Vision International University /Walk in Wisdom Ministries
1115 D Street
Ramona, CA. 92065
1-800-9-VISION
www.drstandekoven.com

For a full list of book titles by Dr. DeKoven please visit:
www.booksbyvision.com
www.drstandckoven.com

Vision Publishing
1115 D Street
Ramona, CA 92065

1-800-9-VISION (984-7466)

www.ingramcontent.com/pod-product-compliance
Lightning Source LLC
Chambersburg PA
CBHW061759110426
42742CB00012BB/2116